T0283912

on track ...
Metallica
every album, every song

Barry Wood

sonicbondpublishing.com

on track ...
Metallica
every album, every song

Barry Wood

sonicbondpublishing.com

Sonicbond Publishing Limited
www.sonicbondpublishing.co.uk
Email: info@sonicbondpublishing.co.uk

First Published in the United Kingdom 2023
First Published in the United States 2023

British Library Cataloguing in Publication Data:
A Catalogue record for this book is available from the British Library

Copyright Barry Wood 2023

ISBN 978-1-78952-269-3

Typeset in ITC Garamond Std & ITC Avant Garde Gothic
Printed and bound in England

Graphic design and typesetting: Full Moon Media

Follow us on social media:
Twitter: https://twitter.com/SonicbondP
Instagram: www.instagram.com/sonicbondpublishing_/
Facebook: www.facebook.com/SonicbondPublishing/

Linktree QR code:

Acknowledgements

Thanks to my pal and fellow scribbler Graeme Scarfe for the inspiration to put pen to paper on one of my true loves. Also, to Leigh Eastwood for igniting the flame during the original Covid lockdowns. To my kids Arran, Ryan, Ruby and Billy – for being with me during part of the writing process and when me and Ruby both tested Covid positive in the summer of 2022 – I love you more than these words can convey.

Thanks also to my Metalli-partners in crime: Phil Dray for that first magical moment, Dale Whorlow for always being on the journey and to my dad, Les Wood and brother Sam Wood – the Metalli-horrors – for the adventures and the gigs.

To my editors, Stephen Lambe and Dominic Sanderson, for the opportunity, pointers and expertise in helping me knock these words into shape – thank you, bosses.

And finally, to Cliff, James, Jason, Kirk, Lars and Robert – Metallica – for being there for as long as I can remember, through thick and thin, highs and lows, good and bad. I wouldn't be half the man I am today without you. The mayhem goes on and nothing else matters... x

on track ...
Metallica

Contents

Introduction

Picture it if you will. A sixteen-year-old me, with my best mate Phil, in a field full of heavy metal fans waiting for their idols to grace the stage. The date is 5 June 1993 (my actual sixteenth birthday), the place is Milton Keynes, UK and Metallica are fast running out of places 'left to roam' on their behemoth of a world tour. This section of the road has been amongst the most lucrative of their careers and they're without doubt one of the biggest heavy metal bands on the planet. But this is not how I first discovered them.

I was sold a couple of years previous when 'Sad but True' and 'Wherever I May Roam' were *heavy* rotations on MTV. 'The Unforgiven' then floored me, especially when the beauty of its classical guitar made way to a sound I'd not previously heard before.

Guns N' Roses, Faith No More, Pearl Jam and Nirvana were already firm favourites, but this was something else entirely. As I was seduced (like so many) by their eponymous 1991 album, their back catalogue duly beckoned, and who could be disappointed with that historic output? Not me and my treasured 'ripped' cassettes, that's for sure.

So, we'll begin here at the beginning, of course, with debut album *Kill 'Em All* – talk about an opening gambit – and push on through a mere 29 more releases, following the ups and downs, the ins and outs and downright heaviness that is Metallica's studio output up to and including the recent *72 Seasons*.

From humble California beginnings, emerging pimple-popped and sweaty out of the global New Wave of British Heavy Metal (NWOBHM) scene in the early 1980s, through to almost complete world domination, sell-out tours and *Billboard*-topping chart success, it's a story like few others and one I hope you'll enjoy journeying with me (yet) again as we peruse a formidable and quite certain, unfinished back catalogue.

Once upon a time, that previously mentioned NWOBHM was flooding the music scene and crossing the Atlantic, and lucky for us, three young Americans and one pro tennis aspiring Dane took the bulls by the horns and gave as good as they could get in order to muscle in on proceedings. Enter Cliff Burton (2.10.62), Kirk Hammett (11.18.62), James Hetfield (8.3.63) and Lars Ulrich (12.26.63).

The latter two had first locked horns in the May of 1981; Lars Ulrich, an insatiable teenage metal fan – borderline fanatic – was already known as a major NWOBHM enthusiast, getting his hands on UK imports almost daily, which eventually led to a hunger to create some music himself. Opposites clearly attracted, and Hetfield's quiet, often insular personality took a suitable back seat to Lars' brash and larger-than-life attitude to metal. The son of a professional tennis player, Lars came from a somewhat privileged background, almost in complete contrast to Hetfield's American working class, run-of-the-mill, blue-collar past.

Their first meeting was a rather uninspiring affair. About to catch a plane to London to try and hook up with fellow NWOBHM wannabes, Lars received a call from someone who'd seen his advert in the LA music paper, *The Recycler*, looking for other musicians to 'jam with': 'drummer looking for other metal musicians/Tygers of Pan Tang, Diamond Head and Iron Maiden'. The caller – an aspiring guitarist named Hugh Tanner – arranged to meet with Lars and also brought his school friend, Hetfield, along with him. Running through a very rough and ready early version of 'Hit the Lights' – the first track off their eventual debut album – all parties were left pretty much non-plussed, with Lars' drumming capabilities still quite basic and Hetfield, as a singer only at this point, delivering a kind of high-pitched falsetto. On his return from Europe, however, Lars called James back and the fledgling wings of Metallica started to flap.

If you're reading this, then you clearly know your stuff; it was bands like Diamond Head, Saxon, Budgie and Iron Maiden who can all squarely be thanked for helping get Metallica out of their garages, onto the road and into a recording studio to put down a blistering debut album in the May of 1983. Before that, there was the small matter of an independently released 'No Life 'til Leather' EP, featuring six tracks that would appear on the debut album – 'Phantom Lord', 'Jump in the Fire', 'Metal Militia', 'Motorbreath', 'Seek and Destroy' and 'Hit the Lights' – along with early track, 'The Mechanix', which would later be slightly rewritten and end up as the seven-minute opus, 'The Four Horsemen'. A special mail-only release, the EP was sent out to fellow eager NWOBHM fans across the world from Lars' bulging contacts book.

The buzz surrounding the EP soon found itself ringing in the ears of record store owner and band promoter Jonny Zazula – who worked tirelessly to wangle Metallica a stint in a 'real' recording studio, set up his own indie label, Megaforce Records, and even secure a contract with UK-based independent label, Music for Nations – to get the album released overseas. And by the time the band hit Music America to lay down their debut album proper, Metallica had already jettisoned original band members, bassist Ron McGovney and lead guitarist Dave Mustaine, replaced by Cliff Burton and Kirk Hammett, respectively.

Hippy Cliff had been poached from fellow San Francisco band Trauma, with a fingerpicking playing style and stage presence of his own. He didn't at first seem a likely candidate; long, messy hair, bell-bottomed jeans and a denim waistcoat. It was his playing that did fit the bill, however, taking influences from musicians such as Jimi Hendrix, UFO's Michael Schenker and Black Sabbath's Tony Iommi, using his bass like a guitar with a distorted wah-wah pedal, he created a sound of his own – the sound of Metallica.

Kirk, originally from high school band, Exodus, learnt his craft by playing along to recordings by the likes of Hendrix, Deep Purple, Black Sabbath, Queen and Status Quo and makes an honest comment on his experience seeing Metallica live for the first time: 'These guys are great, but they could be so much better with me in the band!' He was right.

Metallica are a band of dogged workers. If they aren't on the road, it seems they're in the studio and if they aren't doing either of those, then you'll most probably find them promoting one of these albums. Their incessant hunt for the next loudest, often ground-breaking sound, spurs them on, often ahead of their peers and taking each album on its own merit, heralds progression, experimentation, digression and ... consistency – I couldn't think of another suitable superlative ending in 'ion'.

They rode a wave, then started a tsunami and some of us, well millions actually, have been lucky enough to join them for most of the ride. So, sit back, grab a cup of something hot and/or strong and prepare to be blown away. Metallica give you 'heavy baby!'.

Author's Note
All songs are written by Hetfield/Ulrich, except where indicated throughout this book.

All quotations are taken from Mick Wall's highly recommended and extremely readable *Enter Night – Metallica The Biography* unless otherwise indicated.

Part One: Cliff 'Em All: 1983 to 1986
Kill 'Em All (1983)

Personnel:
Cliff Burton: bass
Kirk Hammett: lead guitar
James Hetfield: rhythm guitar, vocals
Lars Ulrich: drums
Recorded at: Music America, US, May 1983
Producer: Paul Curcio
Release date: 25 July 1983
Chart placings: US: did not chart until 1988, peaking at 120, UK: did not chart
Label: Megaforce (US), Music For Nations (UK)

As first forays go, *Kill 'Em All* stands as a marker in the sand, a bold statement by a group of young metal maniacs who were intent on emulating, then bettering, their musical heroes of the time – think The Beatles' *Please Please Me*, Guns N' Roses' *Appetite for Destruction*, The Sex Pistols' *Never Mind the Bollocks*, Oasis' *Definitely Maybe*, Zeppelin's *Led Zeppelin* and Hendrix's *Are You Experienced* – you'd be hard pushed to convince me it shouldn't be included on that list.

The early hype is well lived up to and they truly arrive with this debut – mainly thanks to Jonny Zazula, whose drive, determination and passion for the music Metallica had to offer helped persuade Music America recording studio owner, Paul Curcio, to record it. Payments were made in instalments – on the proviso that Curcio produced it – with the album eventually costing around $15,000 to make and pushing Zazula to the point of financial ruin for his troubles.

Full of fantastic lyrical imagery, combined with pulsating rhythm guitar, solos and a driving, almost relentless drum and bass partnership – I think the album at least repaid his initial faith. As far as the playing goes, for a rookie band's debut, it's more than impressive. The production is above par – shiny and bright – and the songs are just that, songs that sing. Hummable tunes that burrow into your head, catchy enough to fool you into thinking you've heard them somewhere before, but with just enough musicality to make you want to listen again (and again).

The real 'hit' for me on this album, however, comes with 'Jump in the Fire' (track four) – my pick of the cuts here. Its excellent chorus riffs and the snare drum blasts which introduce them never fail to make me air drum.

There is also an opportunity for Cliff to shine with, wait for it – a bass solo track - and shine he does with some sensational playing. When the drums kick in towards the end, it smacks of a band who are simply letting their (long) hair down, having fun and not giving a damn about anyone else.

The start of side two of the album (from 'Phantom Lord' onwards) heralds a kind of new beginning, often feeling like a different album - two mini-ones released simultaneously if you like. The first side is like an official EP of the early, shorter tracks, with side two showcasing the longer, more complex compositions.

Hetfield said of the record it was 'what we knew – bang your head – seek and destroy, get drunk, smash sh*t up', but the camaraderie was instant – all four band members can hold their own and all shine at moments. The Gary L. Heard album artwork is certainly not to be sniffed at either – intentions are very clear, they're on the hunt for blood. Like something out of a 1980s horror movie (funny that), the hammer and blood stain, along with the soon-to-be familiar lightning effect band logo – in blood red nonetheless – prepares listeners to gird their loins and ears, for what they're about to receive. The back cover photo features all four of our anti-heroes looking suitably baby-faced and angst-ridden too – as was the want of any NWOBHM wannabe archetypes.

We must also not fail to further mention and give a good nod to the aforementioned and illustrious fifth (and not to be forgotten member) Dave Mustaine, who makes contributions to four of the writing credits in the following songs. Though he fell afoul of more than just the band before they hit the studio, his early influence can't be overlooked, especially on 'The Four Horsemen' and 'Jump in the Fire' tracks. Not so much a premature death than a 'Mega' one for him it seemed.

On first listen, you'd be (un)forgiven for thinking the album comes much later in their output. It's an assault on the senses and not for the faint-hearted. Metallica arrive with enough gusto to do exactly what it says on the cover – kill us all ...

'Hit the Lights' (4:17)
From the initial swell of the guitars and Lars' introductory tom fills and tinkling cymbals, Metallica 'flick the switch' on their 'official' recorded releases and one of their first compositions. The intentions are clear from the outset – setting off at a break-neck pace, leaving no holds barred and little room for arguments – they mean business.

'No life 'til leather, we're gonna kick some ass tonight. We got the metal madness when our fans start screaming'. If you were a young metal fan in 1983 hearing this for the first time, I'm quite sure it would have kicked your butt!

The hypnotic riff barely lets up and Kirk's never-ending guitar solo and the track's crescendo finale leave listeners breathless and surely wanting more. A confident and mature start by anyone's standards and a standout track which is angry and assured in all the right places.

This most probably should have been the lead single, particularly as it was one of the first Metallica songs ever written – plus it references the title of that initial EP – but the first single is yet to come and you can't blame them for wanting to try and fan the flames a little more. You'll see what I did there a bit later...

'The Four Horsemen' (7:08) (Hetfield/Ulrich/Mustaine)

The chugging riff panned to the right speaker during the intro shows us that although tender in age, they're not afraid to throw caution to the wind and experiment sonically whenever they can. This track is unrelenting like the protagonists Hetfield screams about – 'horsemen are drawing nearer, on leather steeds they ride, they've come to take your life' – and Lars' double-bass drum pedal work in the verses is a sign of his own prowess to come. The breakdown at just 2:04 in, into the rundown and tempo change, oozes songwriting maturity, with a crowd-pleasing call-and-response penchant fans will grow to know and love. There's some great deft Cliff playing about halfway in and the panned breakdown at 4:58 returns the initial theme again. The payoff is Kirk's haunting solo at 6:23, taking us to the song's frenetic climax. Breathless again and at over seven minutes, it's a good precursor to the longer, more progressive songs that will come to be somewhat of a trademark on their albums in the future.

'Motorbreath' (3:03) (Hetfield)

There's no other way to describe this – a poppy hit every day of the week and I don't care what anyone thinks. It's also (this author thinks) the only Metallica track to have a sole Hetfield writing credit. Lars must have been playing tennis with his dad at the time, although he clearly makes up for it with a brilliant run on the toms in the intro.

The commercial sound of the chorus melody for such a thrashy band cannot be denied. It's like a hint of what their life might have sounded like if they'd stuck this course early on, a bit like how Pink Floyd may have sounded if Syd Barrett hadn't shone so terrifyingly bright.

Hetfield's vocal delivery is right on point, with perfect rhythm and timing, particularly in the verses. The lyrics tell the tale of a young band, living life to the full and going for glory: 'life in the fast lane is just how it seems, hard and it's heavy and dirty and mean'.

'Jump in the Fire' (4:50) (Hetfield/Ulrich/Mustaine)

This is my favourite ever Metallica track and another hit attempt – well, debut single anyway. 'Hit the Lights' apart, as previously discussed, it's still a great choice for a first release; pity it failed to chart anywhere. Featuring another brain-penetrating hypnotic riff, Kirk's end guitar solo is also breathtakingly fast. Their pop sensibility is clearly apparent again in the very commercial-sounding verse and chorus melodies and the 'hooky' trick is Lars' on-point snare drum stabs just before Hetfield launches headlong into the chorus with gay abandon – 'so come on!'. Imagine this track with a drum machine beat and fretless bass playing the main chorus riff – it would surely have been an 80s dance floor classic – that's how catchy it is.

The brilliant Les Edwards single-release artwork depicting the screaming demon also makes this an excellent 'first release' package. A framed 7" picture disc version lovingly adorns my bedroom wall, warding off any potential new girlfriends and assuring my love of this timeless classic and album.

'(Anesthesia) – Pulling Teeth' (3:27) (Burton)

Who puts an annoying bass solo on their debut album? I'll tell you who – Cliff 'toothless' Burton! It's far from annoying, though and lays down another marker that this band are indeed a sum of all the parts. No stars or airs and graces here – they come later, along with the megabucks, limousines and private jets. This track is not all about Cliff either, with Lars getting in on the action too, chiming in on cue at 2:28 – tennis practice over.

It sounds a bit like they think they're on-stage midway through a show rather than recording in the studio – a good nod to the graft that's been put in by the band so far – the toilet circuit and one-man-and-his-dog gigs that had to be chalked off and endured while learning the trade.

It's ambitious anyway and it sets up a fairly ferocious game, set and match to side one, as Lars (again) announces a deadly ...

'Whiplash' (4:06)

The bleed-in intro from the previous track is a stroke of genius as the snare drum fills and guitar stabs announce some impressive, bassy and full-sounding toms. When the main riff kicks in, though, it's quite something to behold and showcases the band's ferocity for the very first time. It's as if they have been holding back a bit on how heavy they can really be – teasing us a little up to track six. Taken in isolation, it also probably best explains what all the initial hype was about. They were sounding quite different to many of their peers at the time – absorbing the vibe of the NWOBHM and using it to create an identity of their own – and this track epitomises it the most.

This 'is' them putting in the shifts at those early gigs – that's this song's very point – and now they really are up on that stage, and you better watch out and protect your bleedin' ears. A crowd-pleaser extraordinaire, which is about just that, pleasing the crowd as they so love to do. 'Hotel rooms and motorways, life out here is raw. But we'll never stop, we'll never quit, cause we're Metallica!'

It's a classic ode to the fans, those very early ones. A tale of a band on the road, playing out their hearts to their adoring fans, the lyrics are vivid, bordering on the comical at times and yet no listener can deny the passion and venom at work here: 'bang your head against the stage like you never did before, make it ring, make it bleed, make it really sore'. It's quite simple really – the fans do it because they adore them – 'cause they're Metallica', obviously.

15

'Phantom Lord' (4:52) (Hetfield/Ulrich/Mustaine)

If you've managed to get your breath back, it's about to be stolen again by another killer riff and deadly drum fill, introducing yet another 'chorus commercial' villain by the name of 'Phantom Lord'. The unusually clean guitar sound following Kirk's echoey lead and breakdown marks a departure – a sign of things to come, perhaps?

Don't worry, though, because the chugging soon returns, with Kirk unleashing the Lord's full might again. We then enter the final verse/chorus run before Hetfield mercilessly bids us to fall to our knees at 4:34. His vocal phrasing is excellent in the choruses again, almost surfing the rhythm of the guitars: 'hear-the-cry-of-war, lou-der-than-be-fore, with-his-sword-in-hand, to-con-TROL-THE-LAND!'. The way he screams the final three syllables sends a chill down the spine. Off with our heads!

'No Remorse' (6:24)

We knew the 'Phantom' wouldn't spare us, and this track proves it. A great protest song, for all intents and purposes, as relevant today as it was back in 1983. War is a subject that they will return to on numerous occasions, indeed, a trilogy of conflict songs awaits us in albums to come – but this one remains on its own, a kind of prologue if you like. It also (once again) shows a maturity in songwriting and structure that paves the way for what's to come. This is not just an album of 'head down, guitars out' three-minute wonders; it's a debut work of art, with intricate playing and carefully crafted suites of music. Something for every metaller to get their heads (banged to) around.

With an exultant 'war without end' cry, Hetfield ushers in a time shift change into a singalong chorus even your grandmother could get behind: 'no remorse, no repent, we don't care what it meant. Another day, another death, another sorrow, another breath'.

At over six minutes long, it's no picnic either, and at 3:47, they flex those deft playing muscles again, all four locked in tight ahead of the final verse. The 'attack' then commences in earnest as the song mutates into a pure thrash-fest to end – 'no remorse' indeed.

'Seek & Destroy' (6:50)

If I referred to 'Whiplash' as a crowd-pleaser previously, then this one takes the biscuit.

From Cliff's majestically trumpeting bass sound in the intro to Hetfield's cool 'alright', which announces it proper – this track oozes metal class. There can't be many Metalli-fans who haven't screamed this chorus out loud in some arena/sports venue/stadium or other over the years – delete as appropriate. It's another near seven-minute opus and the guitars and drums are locked solidly together just before the first verse, coursing together like an impenetrable force.

The guitar run, just after the bridge section, perfectly sets up the chorus melody, giving those fans a chance to shout out: 'searching, seek and destroy!'

At 3:10, they toy with us a little as Lars quickens the pace into an extended instrumental section, with Kirk showing off his lead muscles effectively and when that main riff kicks back in again at 4:13, you can't help but throw a triumphant punch in the air and thank the 'Phantom Lord' you're alive. Another track that epitomises the feel of this debut – contagious, refreshing, ambitious and rewarding – it has it all.

'Metal Militia' (5:11) (Hetfield/Ulrich/Mustaine)
A rather forgotten gem on this album and their entire back catalogue for me, which throws down another gauntlet as if to say, 'if you liked this, then stick around as there's plenty more coming your way'. Hetfield shines vocally, his screech really hitting home, especially on the 'oh through the mist and the madness' parts. They're 'trying to get the message to you', me and anyone else who has the balls to listen.

In a familiar motif, Cliff's impressive bass break at 3:08 lifts the song again as they power through to the end. The marching feet always reminds me of The Sex Pistols' 'Holidays in the Sun' – not bad company to keep if you're trying to make your mark on the world.

Debut done – how will they fare with the 'difficult' second album? We may just have to *Ride the Lightning* to find out ...

Ride the Lightning (1984)

Personnel:
Cliff Burton: bass
Kirk Hammett: lead guitar
James Hetfield: rhythm guitar, vocals
Lars Ulrich: drums
Recorded at: Sweet Silence Studios, Copenhagen, Denmark in the spring of 1984
Producer: Metallica
Release date: 27 July 1984
Chart placings: US: 100, UK: 87
Label: Megaforce (US), Music For Nations (UK)

Released just over a year after that pulsating and passionate debut – they aren't hanging about. Metallica had set a high standard and in doing so, put themselves under quite a bit of newbie pressure. A catch-22 situation in which they needed to maintain their momentum yet surpass their previous effort – no mean feat, but there are worse problems, I guess.

We could have had more of the same. Solid, dependable 'thrash like hell' songs and some of us would have been happy. What we got was all of the above and more, including four six-minute plus sprawlers and one absolute standout back-catalogue classic. A Metallica calling card if you like and probably their most beloved 'greatest (non) hit'.

That songwriting maturity, evident at times in *Kill 'Em All*, is taken up a notch on this album. Some tracks soar, some growl and some scream but with light and shade peppering the album. They break away from the youthful defiance of their debut and grow up in the studio to deliver one of heavy metal's most revered and best-loved works.

The cocky little upstarts even try and produce it themselves, with a little help from Lars' fellow Danish compatriot Flemming Rasmussen (who they'd work with again), revealing a punchier, fatter sound, more aligned to the songs on offer.

Although similar in some respects in style and content to the last one, instead of a 'Whiplash', here we 'Fight Fire'. There's no 'Phantom' but a 'Ktulu' and rather than hitting 'Lights', we 'Fade to Black'. There's lots of melody, too and as Kirk put it:

When the other guys heard the solos on 'Creeping Death' and 'Ride the Lightning', it was a different aspect of soloing than they were used to. Dave Mustaine played fast all the time. I play melodically. And I play parts, different sections that make the solo as hooky as possible.

With *Ride the Lightning*, they suddenly became the *real* Metallica and would retain many of the qualities contained here on future albums. Grandiose and, at times, arrogant, it's almost as if a blueprint is being forged but one with a special ingredient making it hard for any other pretenders to try and dethrone.

Hetfield sounds demonic throughout and the riffs are raucous, this is *Kill 'Em All* up another two notches (at least) in places. But the breathtaking beauty of 'Fade to Black' (track four), with a Hetfield/Kirk guitar duet into a light versus dark first section, shows a versatility like no other, with side one revealing four introductory tracks to rival any of the greatest rock/metal albums.

Lars' performance on this album is the highlight for me, though – impeccable playing from start to finish – and the fact that they even entertain ending their second album with an eight-minute instrumental is preposterous. But when it happens to be of the standard of 'Ktulu', it's even more staggering. It's a monster end to a truly monstrous album.

Three tracks will feature 'heavily' in tours across the next 30-plus years, becoming firm fan favourites and even concert openers – pretty impressive for four new kids on the NWOBHM block. The album artwork, this time derived from the band themselves, is also improved - perhaps one of the most iconic covers of all time - the electric (chair) blue, designed by Ad Artists, is striking, as is the now legendary band logo – standing out in all its 'lightning' glory. The back cover and inner sleeve photos feature the boys in full 'live action' flow, a testament to their early, hectic on-the-road lives.

Crowned the number one Thrash Metal Album of All Time by US magazine Decibel in 2011, back in 1984 they returned with an eight-track wonder affirming their position as a band to be taken very seriously - even if they were still relatively new kids on the 'rock'. We might just be in for a 'shock' here, folks – let's find out ...

'Fight Fire with Fire' (4:44) (Hetfield/Ulrich/Burton)
A. Classical. Guitar.

No, you haven't misheard it – it's there and it's beautiful. But it only lasts for 34 seconds and then they're back. It sweeps in out of nowhere and floors you – one of the most horrific riffs of the 1980s. The band well and truly unleash hell on earth: 'we all shall die!'.

Lyrically, it's a track that is unfortunately as relevant in the global warmth of today as it was back then and musically disturbing too. 'Blow the universe into nothingness, nuclear warfare shall lay us to rest. Soon to fill our lungs, the hot winds of death. The gods are laughing, so take your last breath'.

At 3:30, after Kirk's harrowing, melodic lead break, it drops down to just Lars and his pummelling double bass drum pedals, setting up the final verse/chorus (cue evil laugh of the gods), before a raucous thunder crack and crying guitar bleed magnificently into the title track...

'Ride the Lightning' (6:36) (Hetfield/Ulrich/Burton/Mustaine)
Screeching guitars and a riff of ages announce an epic tale of a man doomed to die in the most inhumane of ways. 'Death in the air, strapped in the electric

chair' – the lyrics are cutting again. But it's the playing that is most impressive here. From 2:22 through to 4:35, it's a constant barrage of guitars and drums. Wave after wave of piercing lead solos sit against a solid backdrop of metal rhythm. You are sat in that chair waiting for the end and you can't escape until Hetfield makes a final plea with the lord – 'someone help me, oh please god help me!' – and we are back to where we started: the 'riff'.

The nightmare eventually ceases when those returning screeching guitars beckon a final, almost thankful, deathly silence.

'For Whom the Bell Tolls' (5:10) (Hetfield/Ulrich/Burton)
The bell rings out and with it comes one of the most iconic heavy metal songs of all time. That 'greatest (non) hit'. It has it all. Driving rhythm, pounding drums and some lead guitar passages that are up there with the very best of them. So why was this not the lead single? The upcoming 'Creeping Death' I can just about understand, though not its spectacular chart flop. But as the bell toll-eth here, then I sincerely hope someone's head did roll in a record company boardroom in early 1985 – a chance missed for sure. If it wasn't considered single fodder, at least it sits very comfortably on the album. Nestled snuggly at track three, it affirms things as business to be reckoned with, with layers upon layers of soundscapes and top-notch playing to discover.

After just two tolls, Lars and Hetfield kick things off before Cliff takes over proper (has to be his melodic invention), plodding us steadily into Kirk's early iconic lead spotlight. The sight of him rocking it out in front of thousands of his adoring public is one most fans have witnessed in person at least once.

The track builds steadily until Hetfield makes it his own in the second verse: 'take a look to the sky just before you die, it's the last time he will'. Then Lars pounds his toms along with the tolling bell (again) as we fade (not to black just yet) into oblivion.

'Fade to Black' (6:56) (Hetfield/Ulrich/Burton/Hammett)
So here we have it. The first track credited to the classic foursome line-up. Soaked in melody, it introduces a brand-new trick up their sleeves – the two (sometimes more) song in one card. It's not a market they grow to corner exclusively, but they do it well and this song is quite possibly their finest example of it. I remember hearing it for the first time – I think it was a live performance – and being staggered. There's real beauty in the sound of the acoustic guitar on this version; the way it almost fades (pun intended) in and complements Kirk's soulful playing. There's a real warmth to Lars' tom sound and Hetfield's vocal delivery is poignant and sorrowful – very believable. 'Emptiness is filling me, to the point of agony. Growing darkness taking dawn, I was me, but now he's gone'.

Let's not forget that this is a band who sang about banging their bleeding heads against full-volume speakers and murderous apocalyptic demons barely a year ago. They soon remind us of that skill set; however when at 3:54, the song mutates into something more familiar – hear the crowd roar as they do. It twists a second time at 4:50 and the balladeering is almost completely forgotten as Kirk works his magical fingers out over the crowd again and fades us to, yes, you've guessed it, black.

'Trapped Under Ice' (4:30) (Hetfield/Ulrich/Hammett)
Flipping the vinyl over starts much the same as side one. Another monster riff, but it has a catchy chorus for such a heavy track. I think, if I'm not mistaken, that's Lars again with the manic double bass drum pedals – practically throughout the entire song. There's also a rather commercial sounding call and response bridge section, 'scream – from my soul. Fate – mystified. Hell – forever more'. It's short and (not so) sweet, but if you think this side of the record is going to follow much the same as the first, you'd be wrong ...

'Escape' (4:23) (Hetfield/Ulrich/Hammett)
Like 'Motorbreath' on the previous album, this has hit single written all over it again. The catchy chorus melody also has some inspiring lyrics as far as usual Metallica fodder goes:

Out for my own, out to be free.
One with my mind, they just can't see.
No need to hear things that they say.
Life's for my own to live my own way.

There's hope here – a chink of light glimmering out of the murkiness of the previous subject matter – but at 2:27, we enter more familiar Metallica fare with a returning tolling bell as things start to get a bit darker. Then at 3:25, a siren sounds to take us into the outro fade – no real return of that catchy chorus, which is a nice twist. They leave it behind almost as if it was a mistake and they didn't mean to turn away from the heaviness so much.

'Creeping Death' (6:36) (Hetfield/Ulrich/Burton/Hammett)
No fear, as the heaviness returns in spades here. The iconic guitar and drum stabs at the start introduce a gothic Phoenician tale of death and destruction which has gone down in the annals of Metallica folklore and will become a live staple – indeed concert opener – for many years to come: 'Now, let my people go, land of Goshen. Go, I will be with thee, bush of fire. Blood, running red and strong, down the Nile. Plague, darkness three days long, hail to fire.' That call and response motif also returns: 'die, by my hand'. This works so well in the live arena, whipping up the crowd into a frenzy and setting up the final verse/chorus section. It's probably this album's pinnacle and as the track comes to an end with those familiar stabs, Kirk wails brilliantly over them, until those Hebrews are dramatically silenced forever.

The sole single release from the album – unfortunately, it failed to chart anywhere.

'The Call of the Ktulu' (8:52) (Hetfield/Ulrich/Burton/Mustaine)

The Ktulu (or Cthulhu if you go by the original name coined by US writer H.P. Lovecraft for his grotesque and hideous maritime monstrosity), is a suitable subject for this lumbering and pulsating album closer.

We had Cliff's 'excruciating' instrumental on the debut album and here we have another – but this time, it's the long haul. Instrumental tracks will play a key role on these early albums and Cliff shines and takes the lead once more here as this track motors along at a steady pace, building and growing as the seconds tick by. It beats and stop/starts like a fractured heart begging for repair.

As the final section approaches, it picks up speed and drives incessantly towards the end – all four playing in unison and locked together – Lars' double bass pedals featuring again before the epic climax. His snare and tom work is also impeccable, hitting them home as hard as he can over some beautiful dual guitar melodies. A live performance of this section (in an album to come) is also exceptional in the way he uses his hi-hat cymbals to express himself. Finally, a clean guitar sound makes a reappearance alongside some menacing kettle drums.

My favourite track on this album – have we 'ridden the lightning'? I'll say, and more.

Master of Puppets (1986)

Personnel:
Cliff Burton: bass
Kirk Hammett: lead guitar
James Hetfield: rhythm guitar, vocals
Lars Ulrich: drums
Recorded at: Sweet Silence Studios, Copenhagen, Denmark from September to December 1985
Producer: Metallica and Flemming Rasmussen
Release date: 3 March 1986
Chart placings: US: 29, UK: 41
Label: Elektra (US), Music For Nations (UK)

There are moments in the tenure of a band which can define them, and the release of this album should be considered one of them. Coming amidst a steady growth in popularity, Metallica were beginning to make a mark – then they released this.

After leaving us practically breathless with their first two albums, one might think they would knock it down a notch for their next offering. No fear of that here – the pace and momentum continue relentlessly.

The title track riff is undoubtedly one of the all-time greats, as is the chorus – anthemic and hugely singable. Hetfield's vocals are more assured, too – gone is much of the shriek, replaced by a gravelly, deeper rasp. The middle guitar section of the song, after the dying cries of 'master! master!...master...' is another highlight.

The melancholic harmonies in the first section of 'Sanitarium' (track four) make it sound suitably haunting and disturbed and with a striking Kirk solo, they end it how 'Fade to Black' should have on the previous album – guitars and drums locked together, right to the death. Speaking of which, there is much of that referenced in the lyrics of 'Disposable Heroes' (track five). A powerful tirade on the futility of war it may well be, but that's not its only muscle. The speed and strength of the playing in the chorus sections is amongst their finest and perfectly encapsulate the horrors, terrors and carnage of battle and conflict.

Yet salvation awaits in the brilliance of 'Orion' (track seven). Another fantastic instrumental with a majestic Cliff cameo in the middle, ushering in some beautiful duelling guitars.

Building on the firming foundations laid with *Ride the Lightning*, it seemed Metallica moved their own goalposts yet again, throwing any kind of formula fans thought they might have understood to the wind. You can almost hear this record thinking and agreeing to itself out loud – 'I've come a long way from those garage rehearsal days.' Bigger and better is also what they delivered. A chart high of 29 in the US and a hair's breadth away from making the UK Top 40 Album Chart.

Alas, the growing fame and popularity did not come without its heart-breaking share of setbacks; on the fateful night of 27 September 1986, while the band were travelling between gigs in Sweden, their tour bus skidded off the road and crashed, killing the legendary Cliff. He was just 24. His loss seemed unimaginable at the time, they were on the crest of a wave, then suddenly cruelly crestfallen. Yet considering *Puppetz* (as the album is affectionately known by both band and fans alike) was to be Cliff's last stand, he didn't half go out on a high. He shines on this record, further underpinning the importance of his creative input and overall impact on the sound Metallica had created up to this point. In only three albums, he had helped to conjure a veritable juggernaut of a band, contributing massively to the quality on offer, most notably to the songs on *Ride the Lighting*. Yet Cliff's crowning glory undoubtedly comes on this release in the guise of his measured playing on the grandiose and previously mentioned instrumental 'Orion' – more of which we'll dissect a little later.

And for this author, a telling 'lump in throat' moment came back in June 2006 when I was lucky enough to witness (along with my father and brother – two other fellow Metalli-lifers) 'the current' band grace the UK Download Festival, headlining for the second time (they've headlined six times so far), on the baking Saturday night. Performing *Puppets* in its entirety from start to finish, amongst other tracks, one could not help but feel the warm ghost of Cliff shining down on the hot and sticky masses who were in obvious raptures.

But back to March 1986 and the album release proper. With a cover destined to grace many a groupie t-shirt, it encapsulates the recorded content with chilling clarity. Don Brautigam's gothic interpretation of the band's and Peter Mensch's (management company Q Prime founder) concept – row upon row of headstone crosses being orchestrated by 'said' puppet master – is striking in its sheer simplicity, yet also classic enough to become a firm fan favourite. The now all too familiar lightning effect band logo also reappears, this time in a haunting marble effect – only adding to the uncomfortable feelings stirred by the surrounding artwork. The back cover features some more, less than elegant live-action band member shots centred around a standard four-piece line-up pose and a cracking stadium shot from Lars' perspective, depicting him raised up from his drum stool, rousing a throng of what looks to be (from a distance) several hundred thousand adoring fans.

Kirk has said of the album:

It was pretty much the definitive musical statement from that line-up, and it felt like it. We had really gotten to know each other's musical capabilities and temperaments ... I could tell that it was really blossoming into something that was to be reckoned with. It was very consistent. Every song we came up with was just like the greatest thing.

Voted number one in Rolling Stones' 2012 readers' poll of the Ten Greatest Heavy Metal Albums of All Time and featuring at a highly respectable, and not to be sniffed at, number 217 in Colin Larkin's extremely readable All-Time Top 1000 Albums from 1998 – let's take a listen and see what strings these master puppeteers can really pull ...

'Battery' (5:10)

As far as opening gambits go, we've already seen that Metallica like to set their stall out early. So far, the downright ballsy 'Hit the Lights' on *Kill 'Em All* – a strong contender for my favourite Metallica album opener – was followed by the dark and deathly shock waves of 'Fight Fire with Fire' on *Ride the Lightning*.

That formula is followed meticulously here again – 'Battery' is what it is – an all-out attack on everything and everyone, but an almost lullaby-esque acoustic guitar in the intro lulls us into that false sense of security before the electric mayhem crashes in. We're then awash with some of the heaviest playing they'd yet committed to tape.

'Smashing through the boundaries, lunacy has found me, cannot stop the battery', Hetfield growls. And he's right; it's quite unstoppable. Especially at 3:48, when there's an almost monster stomp section, all four tightly pummelling their instruments, with Lars destroying his double-bass drum pedals again. It's emphatic playing and you can clearly envisage a frenzied 'Whiplash' of fans lapping this up live.

Speaking of which, it's always a barnstormer when played out to the fans, two performances of which will feature *heavily* in live albums to come.

That monster stomp returns to 'batter' us again at 4:45, mercilessly seeing us out to the end of yet another no holds barred album introduction.

'Master of Puppets' (8:38) (Hetfield/Ulrich/Burton/Hammett)

The title track, but also a signature track. Think of others – Queen's 'Bohemian Rhapsody', Maiden's 'Number of the Beast', Black Sabbath's 'Paranoid', or Motorhead's 'Spades' – it's eight minutes plus of all-time heavy metal and yet it fairly flies by within the wink of a gouged-out eye. The staccato stabs, followed by Lars' snare rolls, introduce a folklore riff.

With a timeless, stadium-bound chorus to boot, the band seem to have really found their feet. They've been teasing us with this – hinting at something majestic to come on their previous output and here they deliver it – with all its pomp and ceremony and soulful, yet very meaty, guitar playing.

With a constant chug of his instrument, Hetfield takes full control of the song and full control of that classic riff – he owns it. Then at 3:29, as his cries of 'master!' echo and distort over some clean picking, it's Kirk's solo that really hits home. Probably my all-time favourite of his. It cries like a petrified baby and so it should do, considering some of the lyrical content on offer here: 'I will occupy, I will help you die, I will run through you, now I rule you too'.

What they started to explore with 'Fade to Black' (the old two-in-one song trick), they accomplish brilliantly here. The 'master, master' call and response section bleeds mercilessly into Kirk's continued petrified playing before dovetailing back into the original verse/chorus section. We end with an almost half-time section before a ring of demonic laughter from 8:15 puts us all out of our misery. Thank you and bad night.

Ask any die-hard Metallica fan what they think of this track – most will tell you it's their favourite – but it ain't mine.

It was brought fully into the 21st-century consciousness thanks to its feature in the Season Four finale of the Netflix smash series Stranger Things, which saw the track hit a peak of number 35 in the *Billboard* Hot 100, and number 22 in the UK Singles Chart in July 2022. Streaming is a 'wonderful' thing, after all.

'The Thing That Should Not Be' (6:32) (Hetfield/Ulrich/Hammett)
Hetfield has widely claimed this to be the heaviest *thing* they've ever written – I tend to disagree. Lyrically dark, sure. Heavy as well, of course – but not 'too heavy man' in my bungled opinion. Perhaps this song is a little sign of how they may have sounded if Cliff had not departed so terribly soon – even though he tellingly doesn't have a writing credit on it.

And exactly what is the *thing* that should not be anyway? Some kind of 'hunter of the shadows', 'lurking beneath the sea' by all accounts. Perhaps we'll never really know, but there's a sure-fire nod to that Ktulu/Kraken creature again and it's a track that features on my Halloween playlist – along with 'Bad Moon Rising' and Stone Temple Pilots' 'Wicked Garden' of course – it's that scary.

Whatever the *it* truly is, it lumbers menacingly out of depths as the chorus takes hold. And with a proper creepy solo from Kirk – like a nightmare you can't escape from – it fits the general horror movie theme uncomfortably well.

'Welcome Home (Sanitarium)' (6:28) (Hetfield/Ulrich/Hammett)
Strategically placed at track four – just like its predecessor 'Fade to Black' on *Ride the Lightning* – I kind of hear these as two peas in a slightly disturbed and most probably decaying pod. The harmonics on the guitar during the intro are a brilliant effect and the early solo just begs to be played out over that stadium sunset on another hot, summer day.

With a lyrical steer towards madness again, I don't think the protagonist in this song is ever really going to make it 'home': 'Welcome to where time stands still, no one leaves, and no one will... Mirror stares back hard, kill is such a friendly word, seems the only way, for reaching out again'.

As the song mutates – again just like 'Fade' – it rocks out like a monster towards the end.

A staple of their live sets, it always brings the houses down. A 'Metallica moment' at all their shows for sure.

'Disposable Heroes' (8:14) (Hetfield/Ulrich/Hammett)

A war protest song – pure and simple – (and won't be their last) but not *quite* that simple on closer inspection. At just over eight minutes long it's another magnificent beast of a track. Incredibly superfast and with some complex playing, especially from Lars – it's relentless throughout – making it my standout track in this collection.

From 1:14, the hell really takes hold as the scything centrepiece riff, along with Lars' precision playing, cuts us down to size. It's not until 1:36 that we get a vocal: 'bodies fill the fields I see, hungry heroes end. No one to play soldier now, no one to pretend' – we know where this one's going then! At 1:57, as the full might of the 'soldier boy' section kicks in, it's like hell on earth. Lars' playing feels like he's aiming straight at you – bullets you can't dodge – and then the masterstroke. After some plaintive playing from Kirk, at 2:32, the catchy chorus trick is back as Hetfield blasts us with the chilling antithesis – 'back to the front' – a cunning wordplay suiting the song's theme perfectly.

This track is so fast-paced that I'm surprised it actually ever gets played live, but has been many times – it debuted at the Metal Hammer Festival in Germany on 14 September 1985 and was last played (at the time of print) at the All Within My Hands, Helping Hands concert and auction streaming event, San Rafael, California on 14 November 2020.

Back to this version, and by the time Hetfield shrieks, 'I was born for dying', I'm pretty sure Lars feels that way too – a dressing gown and shower being the order of the day – 'back to the (dressing room) front (door)', indeed.

Still, they haven't finished us off just yet and we get five final rounds of the breakneck main riff, one with Lars' double pedals and one with him battering his toms to death for good measure. 'Medic!'

'Leper Messiah' (5:38)

This is way heavier than 'Thing': the heaviest thing on offer in this collection in my opinion. I used to think it a bit of an album filler but the sheer heaviness of the riff after the 'bow to leper messiah' lyric makes this far more killer than filler.

During the intro, the listener can be forgiven for thinking the band is about to break out into a slightly jauntier version of 'For Whom the Bell Tolls' from *Ride the Lightning*. As the song settles, however, what we get is a complex track that truly rewards with repeated listens. Not to be skipped. The slightly quickened pace of the 'send me money' section over Lars' pedals works very effectively and adds to the shifting nature of this tale of a demigod who should never be worshipped.

'Orion (Instrumental)' (8:12) (Hetfield/Ulrich/Burton)

Helpfully tagged an 'instrumental' on the album cover and liner notes (as if we couldn't work it out for ourselves), this is another near-end-of-collection monumental finish.

It's a perfect beast, unlike that unsightly Ktulu from *Ride the Lightning*, and has a few quite beautiful moments that again give a knowing nod to their melodic tendencies.

At 3:49, a gothic gong introduces a lovely Cliff solo, leading into a duelling guitar soundscape, transforming what has been a familiar chugging rampage into something completely different. The bass guitar sits exquisitely behind the melodies as we build into a Kirk solo at 6:17 – almost like a love song/ swansong to our beloved Cliff. Memories of that 2006 Download appearance come to mind again when this was performed so brilliantly by the then-band members that day.

We end with a return to the chugging to fade as the track satisfyingly drifts away, continuing the instrumental addition to each album so far.

'Damage, Inc.' (5:08) (Hetfield/Ulrich/Burton/Hammett)
Talk about going out with a bang! Yet the gorgeous reverse bass guitar effect of its opening belies this concluding track's eventual rage and power. Another moment for Cliff to shine and how apt it would turn out to be.

It's not until the 1:19 mark that the raucous riffage resumes, creating a perfect bookend to the 'Battery' opening and the menacingly whispered Hetfield vocal is a great technique employed when uttering the track's title – closing another ever-widening circle of metal for the time being. 'F*ck it all and f*cking no regrets... blood will follow blood. Dying time is here, damage incorporated'.

May Cliff 'pull his teeth' - thank you and RIP - what soon follows is a completely different sound and a completely different band.

Part Two: The Pendulum Swings: 1987 to 1991
The $5.98 E.P. – Garage Days Re-Revisited (1987)

Personnel:
Kirk Hammett: lead guitar
James Hetfield: rhythm guitar, vocals
Jason Newsted: bass
Lars Ulrich: drums
Recorded at: A&M and Conway, Los Angeles, California
Producer: Not Very Produced by Metallica
Release date: 21 August 1987
Chart placings: US: 28, UK: 27
Label: Elektra (US), Vertigo (UK)

After 1986's 'Damage, Inc.' world tour had been so tragically cut short, Metallica found themselves 'helpless' and heartbreakingly bass-less. In true metal-to-leather, dogged fashion, however, they found solace in the one thing they knew Cliff Burton would be proud of them for – making and creating music.

'We needed a place to jam and ended up in a fancy, so-called "real" rehearsal studio. It hella sucked!' – read the hastily scrawled liner notes on the back of this imaginatively titled, *$5.98 E.P. – Garage Days Re-Revisited* release. They needn't have worried, as construction guru newbie Jason Newsted set about transforming Lars' current 'smelly' garage, soundproofing it and making it practice room ready. It turned out to be just like the old days, only with someone brand new and the fruits of their labour were deemed just about good enough to commit to tape.

This collection is a cool bridge between the Cliff years and a 'new Metallica', ready to roam the roads again to see what direction it might take them this time. A direction they set upon after auditioning no less than 40 different bassists in a bid to plug the immense gap left by their former insatiable rhythm section stalwart.

Newsted (3.4.63) had the credentials. Former Arizona-based fellow thrashers Flotsam and Jetsom band member, the chemistry was instant, and the newfound foursome quickly hit the road fulfilling the remaining dates left in the wake of Cliff's passing. Newsted's debut live appearance came on 8 November 1986 at a 'secret gig' at the Country Club in Reseda, California, opening for San Franny buddies Metal Church, another group of thrash metal/NWOBHM architects. Secret the appearance may have been, but the setlist most certainly wasn't. Full of Cliff staples, including both title tracks to *Ride the Lightning* and *Master of Puppets*, as well as early favourites 'Creeping Death' and 'Seek & Destroy', it was some initiation for someone so new and fresh-faced as Newsted.

Continued touring commitments for 'Damage, Inc' went on well into the new year, culminating poignantly back in Sweden at the Frolundaborg,

Gothenburg, on 13 February 1987. With a prestigious booking at the UK's Monsters of Rock bill at Castle Donington secured for later that summer, alongside the likes of Bon Jovi, Dio and Anthrax, and with no new record to promote, time was of the essence.

Covers were key, so dipping back into their heroes' back catalogues seemed a good way to get into the recorded swing of things again, baptise the new boy and set themselves up for the next chapter in their so far, eventful careers. It was also a good way for the rest of the band to battle the loss of their best friend and celebrate his life by playing through and admirably conquering some of the music they'd grown up listening to together.

So, here we have an unlikely collection of early thrash/metal classics, a rogue's gallery if you will, but all of them key in the development and formation of the early direction the band had taken. Diamond Head, Holocaust, Killing Joke, Budgie and the Misfits – not a party for the fainthearted for sure, but one where you're guaranteed a very bad, good time. Don't leave me at the bar on my own for too long, though, will you?

'Helpless' (6:36) (Harris/Tatler)
Originally released by Diamond Head on the *Lightning to the Nations* album, 1980
The live feel start to proceedings soon gives way to an authentic studio sound – impressive when you consider it's 'not very produced' by the band themselves.

It's only right that they kick things off with a Diamond Head track, too – our heroes' all-time heroes. The drum sound is punchy, with Lars' playing also packing some as usual. In fact, they all sound like they're having a damned good time and honouring Cliff in the best possible way.

The original Diamond Head version is a shade more glam than thrash rock, but this humble interpretation begins with some idle band member rehearsal room humming before Lars lets rip and the guitars announce their arrival with that timeless, driving riff.

And at just 2:23, we get a little Newsted solo, cementing his place in the band – the boy can play. Lars re-introduces his double pedals at 3:36 and two savvy time signature shifts take us into another mighty Kirk solo. It's bloody tight.

We end with chugging guitars and stabbing toms to fade, before it's brought back up to the full mix to introduce the next track.

'The Small Hours' (6:39) (Mortimer)
Originally released by Holocaust on the *Holocaust Live – Hot Curry and Wine* EP, 1983
The original 'live' version that this rendition attempts to emulate is a tad quicker – more sinister in its initial vocal delivery too. A menacing 'suck on this' is growled by frontman Gary Lettice, before it truly kicks in.

Hetfield's vocal is performed with far more aplomb, though and he sustains an uncomfortable, unsettling sound throughout where his predecessor failed.

The haunting introductory guitar picking is effectively reproduced in this version, as is the tight snare and bass drum work from Lars. When it fully kicks in, the riff is monstrous and Newsted's fat bassline pushes through the mix towards the end of the verse sections – reminiscent of a certain someone he's humbly taken the place of. A little evil chuckle from Hetfield at 2:24, just after the first chorus, tells us the frontman is enjoying his take on things. At 4:00 on the button, after a longing wail from Kirk's guitar, the pace suddenly quickens with some Lars tom pounding and another exultant, on-beat shout from Hetfield. Kirk's playing is manic as usual here, taking us effectively back into the stomping, steady beat of the final verse to close. We finish with the return of the introductory picking refrain and some more rehearsal room mumblings, rounding off a faithful version of this concert classic. My favourite track on this release too.

'The Wait' (4:55) (Coleman/Walker/Glover/Ferguson)
Originally released by Killing Joke on the *Killing Joke* album, 1980
A fuzzy guitar sound introduces the main riff, then we get a 'one, two, three, four' count in.

There's an interesting vocal effect on Hetfield's verse delivery and his desperate 'wait' chorus call cuts through brilliantly – he's begging for mercy.

The brief breakdown at 2:28 heralds an extended jam section with repeated Kirk solos until that killer chorus returns at 4:19. The feature riff finishes things off proper, but Lars has the final say with a satisfying, echoey snare drum snap.

The original Killing Joke version also has an effect on the vocals, but it's more subtle and not as sinister as Hetfield's take. All in all, a good attempt made, methinks – no complaints here.

'Crash Course in Brain Surgery' (3:10) (Shelley/Bourge/Phillips)
Originally released by Budgie as a 1971 single
There's more 'squawk' than 'tweet' on this raucous retake of the Welsh warblers' criminally insane hard rock classic. The feedback buzz in the intro only adds more authenticity to the live feel of this track and as it kicks in, there's a real sense of festivity – conjuring images of fields full of Metalli-fans moshing to their heart's content on a summer afternoon. The intro showcases more Newsted pedigree as he admirably conquers the opening bass riff, soon locking in with Lars' equally impressive tom tapping. The breakdown at 1:53 is clever, catching the listener off guard. Some reappearing rehearsal room howling, then introduces an impressive Kirk solo, before a second breakdown at 2:33 allows Newsted to shine again. Then it's all over as quickly as it started, ushering in a not-so-lovely two-track finale medley.

N.B. The original version – released as Budgie's debut single in 1971 and not appearing in album format until 1974's *In for the Kill!* – has a real

'Sabbath' feel to it, particularly in Burke Shelley's high-pitched vocal delivery. Then at their own 1:46 breakdown, Robert Plant shows up as they hit pure Zepplin territory.

All things considered, it's yet another fine Metallica cover version, although the original guitar intro does pack a slightly weightier punch than its 'bargain basement' brother, it must be said.

'Last Caress/Green Hell' (3:28) (Danzig)
Originally released by Misfits on the *Beware* EP, 1980 and the *Earth A.D.* album, 1983 respectively

If Budgie can be forgiven for being a little more tongue-in-cheek when it comes to heavy metal, there is absolutely no room for that in these two Misfits mashups. There's also no need to dissect or even repeat those harrowing opening 'Last Caress' lyrics. All diehard Metallica fans know them and have – if we're being honest – secretly regretted singing them loud and maybe not so proud at one point or other. A sure-fire live staple of shows from practically 1987 onwards, it's coupled ingeniously here with the out-and-out breakneck balls of 'Green Hell'. As the 'Caress' fades, its blistering pace and most notably, Lars' insatiable energy, drive us to the end of this chaotic collection of cover versions.

A hilarious (for Metallica) pastiche of Iron Maiden's 'Run to the Hills' is played out to fade at the end. More studio floor shenanigans.

...And Justice for All (1988)

Personnel:
Kirk Hammett: lead guitar
James Hetfield: rhythm guitar, vocals
Jason Newsted: bass
Lars Ulrich: drums
Recorded at: One On One recording studios, Los Angeles, California, from January to May 1988
Producer: Metallica and Flemming Rasmussen
Release date: 7 September 1988
Chart placings: US: 6, UK: 4
Label: Elektra (US), Vertigo (UK)

We've had the knockout debut, the lightning bolt of a second album, and a puppet king pulling all the strings so far.

Momentum gathering momentum until a heart-breaking accident on the road robbed the world of one of metal's most eccentrically unique sounding musicians.

Time waits for no 'heavy metal' men, however, so armed with their newly pressed covers, Metallica hit UK and German summer festivals towards the back end of 1987, appearing alongside Deep Purple and Dio in the latter Monsters of Rock shows at Nuremberg and Pforzheim respectively. A two-night residency at the Troubadour in California in the May of 1988 left a gaping hole in the calendar, so it was back to the studio to lay down their first album proper in more than two-and-a-half years. How to follow *Master of Puppets*? How to continue Cliff Burton's legacy? I don't think any of us were ready for the end result – its sound and subsequent impact.

Think sprawling, epic, progressive heavy metal and this album has it in spades, but gone is the now becoming slightly familiar 'two in one song' card trick. Instead, what we have here is driving, incessant, almost militant riffage, combined with their most politically aware lyrical content yet. Global warming, corporate greed, anti-war sentiments and disturbing insanity pepper this work, but its sound is the most alarming.

This doesn't really sound like the Metallica we've heard so far; it doesn't really sound like Hetfield singing – and where is the bass guitar? The album's overall sound is dry and quite grating at times, with far more top-end than necessary. The drums are also too high in the mix (we know who to blame), with Lars' kick practically sat on your shoulder at times.

As Newsted put it:

I was so in the dirt. I was so disappointed when I heard the final mix. I basically blocked it out ... we were firing on all cylinders ... I was just rolling with it and going forward. What was I gonna do, say we gotta go remix it?

Mike Clink, who'd been drafted in by Lars after his work on Guns N' Roses' *Appetite For Destruction*, put it rather more plainly:

> They weren't leaving enough room ... sonically, to fit the bass in. But that was their concept and I think that if Cliff had been there, it might have been a bit different.

Clink was later credited for helping out with the drum tracks on two of the songs on the album, 'Shortest Straw' (track five) and 'Harvester of Sorrow' (track six). Nevertheless, what this album lacks in produced sound quality, more than makes up for in the compositions offered. It rocketed into the Top Tens of both the US and UK charts and features a track which would secure them in the annals of heavy metal history forever. Most notably 'One' (track four), their highest charting single so far – 13 in the UK – and for many, I'm sure, considered the most iconic Metallica track of them all. Helped, of course by the incredibly MTV-unfriendly and emotive music video to accompany it. 'One' also later went on to win the first ever (1990) Grammy Award for Best Metal Performance – another nod at their now steady rise to wider fame and notoriety. You can keep your (impending) sandmen and your sanitariums, your puppets and bells – it surely is the 'One'. The sheer force and aggression of the second stage of the song – the 'absolute horror' – encapsulates it all. Melody, power, storytelling, incredible musicianship and an insane guitar solo – but more of that later.

There is no doubt though, that this is the worst overall sounding of all the Metallica albums. Dry as a bone, with too much drums and bass guitar criminally lost – there are many faults to pick at. Call it self-indulgence, band member pecking order or downright arrogance. I put it down to a band having to almost completely transform themselves, deal with huge grief, contractual commitments, a hectic schedule and the impending loom of fame. Some or all of the above are bound to have an effect on the dynamics and output of any band.

The album's cover artwork, the concept of Hetfield and Lars, is realised brilliantly by Stephen Gorman's gothic depiction of a battered and bruised poor old Lady Justice. The back cover features untypical mugshots of all four band members, with Newsted looking slightly nonplussed – new boy having doubts, perhaps? No wonder if he can't hear his own instrument. He got the chance to work out any musical frustrations on the road as it happens, as after those previously mentioned first two shows in 1988, the band locked horns with rock gods Van Halen, who were running their own rather ostentatious 'Monsters of Rock' tour. This culminated on 30 July at the Mile High Stadium in Denver, Colorado, before Metallica's Damaged Justice tour kicked off in Budapest, Hungary's MTK Stadium on 11 September, a show which featured no less than five of the total nine *Justice* cuts – four of which were played for the very first time that night.

The tour ran until 7 October 1989, with 220 shows across the world, including South America, Australia, Japan, New Zealand, Europe and extensive US dates. Did the music do 'em justice – let's find out.

'Blackened' (6:40) (Hetfield/Ulrich/Newsted)

For all intents and purposes, this can be defined as a ballad – an ode to Mother Earth – albeit a dark and brooding one, full of anger, resentment and rage. A rage that takes a little while to manifest once again, as the now familiar and trademark lullaby-esque album intro breaks out into a barrage of guitar and drums at just 36 seconds. It's then that the 'new' sound hits home – like a sledgehammer. But it's tight and pacey, with a great riff and Lars' kick drum right in your chest. At 1:13, the core of the song is unleashed, with the chugging guitars sitting wonderfully beneath a now more deepened Hetfield growl than we've previously been accustomed to. At 1:36, the introductory riff returns, but the song takes an almighty if not catchy twist here: 'Fire, to begin whipping dance of the dead, blackened is the end', Hetfield roars as Lars pummels the double kick. It's a commercial melody and the final chorus call of 'colour our world blackened' begs that stadium crowd singalong again.

At 2:34, the stadium vibe gets cranked up another notch, with another riff coupling effectively with Lars' snare stabs this time. Hetfield's single-word, almost call-and-response vocal technique bleeds into the true meaning of this track: 'See our mother (earth), put to death. See our mother die'. A blistering, seemingly never-ending solo from Kirk then screams out, bringing us into the final verse/chorus run. The earth is then silenced emphatically as the song stops abruptly to let us draw breath.

'...And Justice for All' (9:44) (Hetfield/Ulrich/Hammett)

A clean, almost gentle guitar sound kicks off this monster title track and at well over nine minutes, it's another strap yourself in and prepare for the best/ worst scenario.

Lars' snare drum might sound a little dry, but he uses it to great effect 56 seconds in when four separate stabs build the momentum to lead us into the song proper. It's also here that we might begin to understand why the drums feature so high in the overall album mix. They are integral; they drive this song and keep it motoring along, especially from 1:13 ahead of the main riff. The toms sound great – punchy and clear, pairing effortlessly on the beats with the main riff. It's not until 2:11 that the vocals kick in – that's one hell of an intro! By now, Hetfield's newfound growl sounds measured and assured – like he's always sung in this way. As we approach the chorus, that commercial sound returns: 'seeking no truth, winning is all, find it so grim, so true, so real'. The four snare drum stabs then reappear to take us satisfyingly into the extended solo from 4:52, Kirk wailing desperately just before the verse riff kicks back in at 5:54. Things then slow down a little to take us into the business end of the track, with the intro melody now being played by that familiar chugging, rhythm guitar. Hetfield has his final say, spitting out the chorus lyrics with real aplomb. Justice done? I'll say.

'Eye of the Beholder' (6:25) (Hetfield/Ulrich/Hammett)

Released as the second single (US only) on 30 October 1988, this track sums up that new Metallica sound, indeed the overall sound on this album, this fan feels.

It's a brooding beast of a track and comes rumbling out of the wreckage they left Lady Justice reeling from. Lars' floor toms sit perfectly underneath the rhythm guitars, his snare drum used to great effect again to emphasise the beats of the verse. Then his military precision fill launches us headlong into the song proper. At 45 seconds in, all the instruments (yes, even the bass) are locked solidly together, so tight it sounds like they can never be parted. The reason behind its surprising choice as a single release (even though it failed to chart), must be squarely down to the catchiness of the chorus sections: 'Doesn't matter what you see, or into it what you read, you can do it your own way, if it's done just how I say', dictates Hetfield in a singalong section.

A nod goes to Kirk's soulful solo on this track, too, particularly at 4:57 – it's played with so much feel and parallels Hetfield's rhythm guitar perfectly. The progressive nature of this track, coupled with its more commercial-sounding elements, makes this my favourite from the album. It brings all the previous elements of their songs together in – 'one'. Speaking of which ...

'One' (7:24)

As the bullets and explosions spray across the speakers and the helicopter pans right to left, something tells us we're in for something a little different here. And when that clean guitar chimes in at eighteen seconds, it truly arrives – it's haunting. The little lead melody over the top soon after is akin to Pink Floyd's 'Wish You Were Here' intro, but when the acoustic guitar bleeds out over the introductory chorus section, it's a thing of real beauty.

Lars' kick drum is a little too overpowering in these sections, but his real trick on this track is yet to be revealed. Hetfield's vocal delivery is plaintive and wholly believable, with a lovely tone – 'fed through the tube that sticks in me, just like a wartime novelty' – the horror is being revealed. A woeful cry of 'please god, wake me' echoes out to introduce a perfectly understated guitar solo before 'please god, help me' is uttered. Now the marching feet are firmly planted in our chests thanks to Lars' incessantly pounding double kick drum pedals – played with real precision. Then at 4:36, everyone's locked in tight, rhythm guitar furiously lashing against the drums as we enter the real crux of this integral Metallica tune: 'Darkness – imprisoning me. All that I see – absolute horror'.

At 5:28, Lars riddles us with snare drum bullets, and we understand the true horror of war. It's brilliantly interpreted, Metallica using their heavy metal art form in the most explosive fashion. Lars hasn't finished with us yet and after a chaotic Kirk solo, those snare drum bullets morph into tom bullets as he attacks his kit with breath-taking force at 6:22. This section of the song immerses the listener in a combative barrage of sounds; there is no escape from it until those cymbal crashes allow us an escape route at 7:18. Then silence...

As ambitious a track as they have attempted so far. This was the third single from the album, charting at number 35 in the US and that very respectable 13 in the UK. Now they had arrived.

Scooping that previously referred to debut Grammy in 1990, it's a tune that's proved integral to their live sets for the last 30-plus years. An absolute showstopper every time.

And that video I mentioned earlier – another first for the band – premiered on MTV on 20 January 1989, shot almost entirely in black and white and featuring dialogue from the anti-war film *Johnny Got His Gun*. It brought them to the attention of the masses and more. 'One' to watch now, for sure.

'The Shortest Straw' (6:35)

After such an emotional, hard-hitting, heavy metal rollercoaster, we're thrust straight back into more standard Metallica fare here.

The messy, stop-start intro belies this track's true theme when the main chorus riff kicks in after just fourteen seconds. At 46 seconds, it takes another surprising turn with a fast-paced verse melody skilfully handled by Hetfield and Lars' double kicks echoing the lyrics – 'deafening' – at 1:25.

The guitar solo builds menacingly after the chorus from 3:46, then stops abruptly to take us back into the final (verse/chorus) stages of the track. The problem with this song is that it does go on a little bit – bordering on the annoying at times – but any track coming after the previous 'one' was probably always set up for a fall. It's the clearest example on the album of where the production seriously lets things down. There are no dynamics and you're left wishing it would end sooner.

'Harvester of Sorrow' (5:42)

The first 'internationally' released single from the album and a pleasing No.20 in the UK, which is surprising considering the lyrical content on offer here: violence, drugs, alcohol... infanticide! This is a Metallica stalwart, though – a hundred times better than the short straws before it – with energy that comes across most effectively when played live. There's deep-rooted evil in that introductory guitar-picking melody and when Lars pounds the toms and kick drum, a beast of epic proportions is fully unleashed.

I can imagine many a parent being thoroughly unimpressed – scratch that – horrified, on hearing this ringing out of teenage bedrooms in the late 1980s, but that undermines the quality of this track. 'All have said their prayers, invade their nightmares. To see into my eyes, you'll find where murder lies'. This is very dark matter, worryingly so if you try to read too much into it – but perhaps that's the point.

Lyrics aside, we're now six years on from that first batch of bashed-out *Kill 'Em All* tracks – four albums in too. The assuredness and downright 'f*ck it all' confidence this track oozes can't be denied. It pins listeners to the wall and demands attention – rock and roll in its truest and darkest form – and they don't give a damn.

N.B. a definitive live release (part one of the upcoming international 'Sad but True' single) can be found in the performance taken from the band's appearance at the Tushino Airfield, Moscow, Russia, on 28 September 1991, as part of the Monsters of Rock tour alongside AC/DC, The Black Crowes and Pantera. The crowd were in a savage mood and this version of the song did little to quell their excitement. Just listen to Hetfield's antagonistic hell cry of 'come on!' at 2:56 if you need further evidence. Chaos.

'The Frayed Ends of Sanity' (7:40) (Hetfield/Ulrich/Hammett)
The demons abound in this track, niggling away at the threads of our mentality – just as its title suggests. You can even hear the devil's henchmen themselves - during the first 30 seconds before the main riff kicks in – see them pacing the corridors of hell.

Hetfield's vocal is strong, particularly in the chorus sections – his new 'gruffer' tone suiting these more compact, direct, one-trick numbers. The little drum breakdown just after 4:00 introduces a neat (second) solo section, Kirk screaming out over a solid bed of rhythm guitars. Another stop-start at 5:48 then takes us satisfyingly into a final verse/chorus run to end – with a suitably demonic Hetfield laugh to finish us off. Not as strong (again) as the track before it – but much better than 'Shortest Straw'.

'To Live is to Die' (9:48) (Hetfield/Ulrich/Burton)
...and out of the insanity emerges more beauty – those wonderfully chiming acoustic guitars again – but only for about a minute before they make way for the usual metal mayhem. It's nicely done, though, and this extended instrumental is a pleasing addition to the set, with more than one surprise along its mammoth route.

The slight time change shifts, particularly in the run-up to the first solo, are really effective, helping the track maintain its momentum. Kirk's guitar sounds vibrant and on point before a cleaner one, then changes tack a little – this is different sounding, older territory. Burton's writing credit is not to be overlooked here; he's still a massive loss. The spoken word lyrics, that come out of nowhere, are a surprise addition too: '...all this I cannot bear to witness any longer, cannot the kingdom of salvation take me home...'. They almost seem out of place, but as the heaviness drifts away again, the shimmering acoustic guitar returns to bookend us nicely.

'Dyers Eve' (5:12) (Hetfield/Ulrich/Hammett)

There is no let-up as this final track hits home, coming straight off the back of the one before. Lars' echoing tom run bleeds effortlessly into a fast-paced, hell-for-leather stomper from 36 seconds. Those trusty double-kick drum pedals completely floor us throughout the entire verse sections, which seem to go on forever, but it's far from annoying this time. Kirk tries to have the last say, though, going out with an almighty bang at 3:37 and before we know it, the whole thing's over ...

Whatever next, then? Well, that impending fame I mentioned earlier is about to hit hard – very hard indeed. Next, we find out what the Metallica of the 1990s sounds like.

Metallica (Black Album) (1991)

Personnel:
Kirk Hammett: lead guitar
James Hetfield: guitars, vocals
Jason Newsted: bass
Lars Ulrich: drums
Recorded at: One On One recording studios, Los Angeles, California, between
October 1990 and June 1991
Producer: Bob Rock, with Hetfield and Ulrich
Release date: 12 August 1991
Chart placings: US: 1, UK: 1
Label: Elektra (US), Vertigo (UK)

The Damaged Justice tour came to an end in Brazil on 7 October 1989, and
with only a handful of dates pencilled in for the following year, the band
regrouped, rehearsed and eventually reinvented themselves yet again with
the release of their fifth eponymous album – referred to by many as simply
the *Black Album*. As simple as the cover artwork may have been – an almost
hidden classic band logo, with a coiled snake gracing the bottom right
corner against pure black – there is nothing simple about the twelve tracks
which ring out as needle hits vinyl here. They had surely learnt a lesson too,
drafting in Bob Rock (Mötley Crüe/Bon Jovi/Aerosmith) on production duties;
gone is the rasping dryness of *Justice*, replaced by a warmer, fatter, more
melodic sound, also more akin to the sounds of the early 1990s, as classic
rock began to seriously overtake the airwaves and send a new generation of
long-haired teenagers into raptures.

Hitting the number one spot on both sides of the Atlantic and selling multi-
millions in the process, the album spawned no less than five singles (two UK
Top 10s) and sparked their biggest tour(s) to date – 'Wherever We May Roam/
Nowhere Else To Roam' – running from 29 October 1991 to 4 July 1993.

A lot of what's contained here is radio-friendly fodder and that's not
necessarily a bad thing. From garage days, they've come, building steadily
along the way. Now the core writing partnership of Hetfield and Ulrich has
the confidence to push the heavy metal boundaries safe in the knowledge that
their ardent base of fans will embrace and respect a less familiar flavour from
now on – no more nine-minute opuses, with breakneck, finger-numbing solos
then. What we get is more standard rock and roll, yet still retaining the dark,
progressive edge which clings firmly to their metal roots. As Lars himself put it:

They were all different from each other (previous albums), but they were all
going in the same direction … long songs, longer songs, even longer songs.
It was time to take a sharp turn. The only way to do that would be to write
one long song to fill the whole album or write songs that were shorter than
we had done before. And that's what we did.

With a more 'live' feel to proceedings this time out, producer Rock stamped his authority on the sessions by urging the band to play together in the studio, rather than put their tracks down separately. Take after take was attempted, aborted and attempted again to try and get the best possible version of each song. A formula that clearly paid off, as on release, Rolling Stone magazine gave it a five-out-of-five-star rating and later included it in its 'essential recordings of the 90s' list. It also won them another Grammy in the Best Metal Performance category again and was the band's first album to debut at number one in the US album charts.

So call it 'what you will', the 'Black' album, the 'snake one', self-titled or what I think it should be called: simply 'Metallica' – this was a game changer beyond all imagination.

The 'Sandman' (track one) intro is one of rock's most infamous, the signature guitar picking into the riff and drums. Finally, we get to hear Newsted's bass as the verse bursts into life and Hetfield unleashes his now trademark growl. With a sing-a-long chorus and effective 'now I lay me down to sleep' spoken word section, it's little wonder it was nominated for a Grammy in '92, criminally losing out to Sting's 'Soul Cages'.

After a spate of iconic radio-friendly tracks - 'Sad but True' (track two), 'The Unforgiven' (track four), 'Wherever I May Roam' (track five) - they then go a bit political with the deadly sounds of 'Don't Tread On Me' (track six), then commercial again with 'Through the Never' (track seven) that will always sound at home on the radio – late night rock show naturally.

Then comes another bonafide, 100 per cent guaranteed changer to end all games.

When the open strings of 'Nothing Else Matters' (track eight) are delicately picked, an entirely new door is gently nudged ajar. One which entices a multitude of new ears. Ears which previously might never have given Metallica a second listen now seem pricked and interested.

And how do they repay these newly invested followers, those recruited off the back of what is a soft metal ballad? With a typically rousing tune about the primal instincts of mankind, of course! 'Of Wolf and Man' (track nine) practically sums up what this band has been about for the past four albums. It also shows the confidence, almost arrogance, of a band who know they can still flex their muscles when required but also have the versatility to (shape) shift moods and styles – no full moon required.

I think what's most telling about the next two tracks is the fact that they both begin with and continue to be driven by strong bass lines. After what's previously occurred, it's a real nod of approval to the new boy and almost feels like a public apology. They also show the progressive and evolving nature of the band, a hint of what's to come and what more they have to offer. If you'd bought this album as a new fan solely off the back of one of the singles and were left a bit nonplussed by 'Tread' or 'Wolf', then 'God That Failed' (track 10) and 'My Friend of Misery' (track 11) definitely proved your money was well spent. Yet the album ends as if they are the Metallica of the past again. With 'Struggle Within' (track 12) sounding like it could be at home on *Ride The Lightning* or *Puppetz*.

By the time they finished touring it, they were practically household names – forever etched in the echelons of heavy metal history. Is it because the material is more accessible to the average music-buying general public? Or simply down to the fact that they know how to craft the almost perfect five-minute-ish heavy rock track? A little of both is what probably ticked most of the boxes here. Whatever the real reason for its far-reaching global success, its impact cannot be overstated and by the end of the aforementioned, gut-wrenching tour, it had catapulted them into the rock mainstream – making them a force to be reckoned with from hereon in. It was a time when rock was king and with bands like Guns N' Roses, Aerosmith and Def Leppard now dominating MTV playlists with their new blend of stadium-friendly singalong anthems, not ones to be left standing, Metallica were in it to win it too and back to black. With a catalogue that would prove to stand the test of time, they brought heavy metal screaming from its humble and thrashy 1980s beginnings into the back end of the 20th century, 'through the never' and beyond.

'Enter Sandman' (5:29) (Hetfield/Ulrich/Hammett)

From the moment the iconic picked riff begins, we 'enter' new territory. The first single from the album – the only first choice lead single, really – heralds a new sound, a new direction, a new band. A sound like nothing that's come before it and that will define them as they continue to forge their new metal direction. This is a more accessible sound all round and although there is no sneaking hush like on all the previous album starts – clean guitars announce this long player – the attack is no longer instantaneous. There is now some measured consideration, with an extended, building intro adding a new air of intriguing anticipation to this collection.

And do you hear that? That's a bass guitar, that is. Not hidden away under a mass of guitar and drums anymore, but a living, breathing, rumbling beast, underpinning everything else and holding it all together. This is how it should sound – well done that Bob.

The production allows the music to breathe, and Lars' typically tight playing lends itself wonderfully to this exciting, clever and lyrically accessible composition.

It's a theme we're all familiar with at one time or another in life – the threat of a nightmare and being woken by something terrible that's lurking under the bed. We need to hold those sheets close to our eyes too, as come 55 seconds in, this monster track kicks in full pelt – 'say your prayers little' ones.

The chorus is as catchy as they come and certainly as catchy as anything they've penned to paper so far – screaming into the UK Top 10 at No.5 – their highest-ever place - and hitting a very respectable number 16 in the

US. It even has a trademark Kirk solo. But at 3:18, as it breaks down just before the main riff again and we hear the terrifying spoken word section, we really do break through into new, uncharted Metallica territory: 'Now I lay me down to sleep, pray the Lord my soul to keep. If I die before I wake, pray the Lord my soul to take'.

First played live at the Phoenix Theatre in Petaluma, California on 1 August 1991, and forever destined to grace the stage and many a rock covers band's set list (including my own) from here to eternity.

'Sad but True' (5:24)

As we wake from one nightmare, so another is unleashed upon us here in the form of a tale of true woe – a man consumed by inner demons, whispering voices, insecurity and paranoia. Standard fare for a Metallica track, then. Maybe not so much for one of the singles from the album, though, albeit the final one, released on 8 February 1993, including that previously mentioned Moscow version of 'Harvester of Sorrow' – shame it hardly dented the single charts (US: 98, UK: 20). Considering they'd been touring the hell out of the album, they weren't even into the back end of the 'Roam' tour on its release, its relative chart failure is somewhat of a mystery. Or maybe, like the band, the singles-buying general public were beginning to have enough of this mega *Black Album* after all.

Nonetheless, it's a standout track, hooky in all the right places, mainly thanks to Lars' impeccable playing. The tight drum sound, staccato stabs and stop-start arrangement hammer home this track which yearns to be played at full volume. The complete dead stop at 3:05, before the guitar solo, seems to hang forever and the final 'hate, I'm your hate', at 4:16, emphasises the song's true sentiment.

The structure of this track screams out as a direct nod and appeal to the MTV culture of the 90s – straightforward verse, bridge, chorus, instrumental, repeat – with the band now seemingly more than happy to reach out to a new cohort of more commercially aware fans, making its mediocre chart performance all the more puzzling.

'Holier Than Thou' (3:47)

An extended heavy riff introduces us to track three. They're rumbling along nicely now as the album cranks up a gear. During (the end of) the recording sessions, it was widely reported that Bob Rock suggested this be the lead single. Were it not for the obvious choice of 'Sandman' – sure-fire suicide it would have been to overlook it – it may well have been a good shout. With a driving rhythm, brain-numbing riff and singalong chorus, it would have no doubt set down a marker in the sand(man) and put those few fans, who were becoming concerned about this new direction the band were taking, at ease. What this track also has is a fantastic lead break from Kirk and wait for it – a bass spotlight. There it is at 3:12 taking us to the song's climactic end.

Sounding fat and full of life, Newsted has also truly arrived, and he sounds like he's finally enjoying recorded life. No more of that dry *Justice* sound.

'The Unforgiven' (6:26) (Hetfield/Ulrich/Hammett)

From one extreme to the other, it seems, as when that hornpipe-like sound ushers in the majestic acoustic guitar, heads are turned. They have our full and undivided attention.

Whenever I hear this track, I'm transported back to that teenage version of myself I mentioned in the introduction of this book. I had never heard anything so beautiful, so haunting, so different. The extended intro here, with that soulful, mournful guitar, suddenly makes way to an excruciating wall of sound like no other. Hetfield's vocal melody is at one with the hypnotic rhythm guitar – they're inseparable. Lars' drums are on absolute point yet again, but not overpowering like on the previous album. This time they sit majestically beside the other instruments, binding the overall sound together and accentuating the composition in all the right places. When the chorus hits, the beauty is fully realised; Hetfield's most poignant vocal delivery yet – 'so I dub thee unforgiven'.

Kirk's solo soars out of the speakers, lifting the track to new heights, preceded by – yes, you've guessed it – those pinpoint, accurate drums again.

The final two minutes then lull us into a never-ending rapture with the final chorus refrain looping over and over to fade (to black and beyond).

The album's ambitious second single (US: 35, UK: 15).

'Wherever I May Roam' (6:42)

With a gush of Eastern promise, a tale of life on the road is about to unfold.

The *Black Album* tour was all-encompassing – a total of 291 worldwide dates – but this was written long before they'd roamed the planet promoting this latest offering. Still, they knew what they were talking about, cutting their teeth on the tour bus up and down respective countries, honing their craft and playing abilities in no better way.

The snare drum signals in a riff of power as the monster is unleashed and then as the main riff settles, Lars explores the kick and floor toms as only he knows best during the verses. The chorus has that familiar singalong feel 'anywhere I roam, where I lay my hat is home' after Hetfield spells out exactly what this merry band of men have been all these years – 'rover, wanderer, nomad, vagabond' – all of those and more.

The guitar solo complements the chorus chords brilliantly, then turns on a sixpence and wails out over the verse sections again. Hetfield goads us to the end and whips up that stadium crowd again, too – 'wherever I may wander, wander, WANDER!' Sounding as good as this, let's hope they don't wander too far out of earshot from now on.

The album's penultimate single, and my favourite track on the album, this time a disappointing US: 82, but with a more respectable UK: 25. I consider myself a contributor to its UK chart position as it was the first Metallica CDS I bought, and it still sits proudly on my shelf with my Milton Keynes ticket stub stuffed safely inside. At just track five, we've also had four of the album's five single releases so far. A strong catalogue and we're not even halfway through.

'Don't Tread on Me' (3:59)
When this track was penned, the world was coming to terms with the duration and subsequent aftermath of the Gulf War. As tongue in cheek as the introductory guitar refrain is – a nod to 'America' from the musical West Side Story – the lyrics pack more of a satirical punch than ever. A 'f*ck you', 'don't mess with us' approach is boasted throughout – 'liberty or death, what we so proudly hail, once you provoke her, rattling of her tail. So be it, threaten no more, to secure peace is, to prepare for war'.

The monstrous guitars of the verse sections perfectly fit the bill; this is as heavy as anything they've released and the guitar solo at 2:33 is as evil as they come. The snake on the album cover has been rattled and is about to bite down hard.

'Through the Never' (4:01) (Hetfield/Ulrich/Hammett)
With a riff more akin to those *Kill 'Em All* days of yore, this track comes screaming out of the never. But it also showcases the band in all their 'current' glory. Still able to pack a punch, but with a melodic sensibility, they've learnt to craft with the best of them. The breakdown from 2:47 expresses this clearer than ever with another call and response section any crowd would relish: 'On. Through. The. Never. We must go on. Through. The. Never'. The hooks are piling up quicker than a US public holiday fishing trip.

'Nothing Else Matters' (6:29)
To call this track pivotal probably still underplays it a little. They've toyed with this formula before – think 'Fade to Black' from *Lightning*, 'Sanitarium' from *Puppetz* – but they've never seen it through until now.

The simplistic genius of the introductory guitar picking is double-stamped by the melodic beauty of the lead pattern before you are engulfed by a flush of strings and you wonder exactly where those Gulf War brutes have vanished to.

Hetfield's 'unforgiven' soul has returned as he croons through the verses with consummate ease. Lars peppers them with an understated groove, never overpowering, never trying to steal the show – just letting us know he's always there. We think it's going to build, but they fool us as we enter a hushed solo section. But wait, we're building again, and from across another rousing bridge, it comes with all its force. Roaring at us like the monster it's been suppressing, all the hairs are on end as it sweeps us firmly off our feet. Then just like that, the quietness returns. A musical masterstroke cramming all that we love best about this band into six-and-a-half minutes.

'Couldn't be much more from the heart'. No, it couldn't. It also couldn't be further from those days of thrash either, but we like it. And we like it A LOT.

The third single from the album, securing a number six in the UK chart, their second highest so far. New fans, new fame. 'Nothing' will ever quite sound the same again – thank God.

'Of Wolf and Man' (4:16) (Hetfield/Ulrich/Hammett)

Now the monster does roar – but this is no wolf in sheep's clothing. The deafening intro stabs leave us in no uncertainty here; they're back to their basic best as Hetfield vocally blasts us into oblivion. He summons the beast in death-defying fashion at 3:17, guitars howling underneath a spoken word section – that's two on this album – as the sounds erupt around us: 'so seek the wolf in thyself'.

It's frightening, animalistic and of course, is on my Halloween playlist, naturally. The return of the introductory stabs 'shape shift' us back into silence as the song mercifully comes to an end and the nightmare is over, for now.

'The God That Failed' (5:05)

Bass guitar is king again here, as we enter the album's final stages. Newsted shines through bold and bright alongside the chiming guitars in the intro before Lars announces the riff proper with a flourish of that dependable snare drum.

There's not much hidden in this track, but an extended solo section allows all band members to flex their respective muscles, before a complete breakdown at 4:00 exact – including a triumphant Hetfield studio yell – sets us up for the finish. A satisfying, surprisingly clean guitar strum for good measure to end.

'My Friend of Misery' (6:47) (Hetfield/Ulrich/Newsted)

Newsted is back setting the scene, this time with a writing credit too, handling things well as the melodic tones of his bass guitar sweep us almost gently into the song proper. The guitar riff sits nicely on top and it's just over a minute before any vocals kick in at all.

Speaking of which, the chorus vocal melody dovetails pleasingly with the solid guitars – surfing the beat – before Newsted's bass bubbles back to the surface to begin verse two. I think that's a cowbell I hear as well?

At 3:13, the track breaks down to another extended solo section, this time for the bass. As Newsted lays the foundations, an echo of guitars weave in and out of him. A harmonic lead break then allows Kirk to take over, his 'wah wah' sound now mopping up the spaces left between the chorus riff. As the track comes to a close, Lars double-times things, quickening the pace a little before it settles back down to finish.

'The Struggle Within' (3:51)

A militaristic drum pattern announces the final song of the album – with more pomp than ceremony, as this short and sweet track soon reveals.

Newsted has left it late to get in on the full proceedings, but he's here again, this time piping up on backing vocals to ably aid Hetfield deliver this vitriol of internal hate: 'Home is not a home, it becomes a hell. Turning it into your prison cell. Advantages are taken, not handed out, while you struggle inside your hell'.

A final flourish of Kirk's lead guitar takes us into the final minute – but not before Hetfield yells 'go!' as the final chorus refrain is brought to a thunderous stop by the guitars and snare drum working as one.

So how on earth do you follow that? You tour it to absolute death and then regroup before churning out a 14-track, thrash-less opus - that's how.

Part Three: Time to Reload: 1993 to 1999

Live Shit: Binge & Purge (1993)

Personnel:
Kirk Hammett: guitar
James Hetfield: guitar, vocals
Jason Newsted: bass
Lars Ulrich: drums
Recorded at: The Sports Palace, Mexico City, on 25, 26, 27 February and 1 and 2
March 1993, the Sports Arena, San Diego, California on 13 and 14 January 1992
and the Seattle Center Coliseum, on 29 and 30 August 1989.
Producer: Hetfield and Ulrich
Release date: 23 November 1993
Chart placings: US: 26, UK: 54
Label: Elektra (US), Vertigo (UK)

What follows the biggest tour of the band's career? A live album chronicling
said tour of course – it had to come. The format of this first 'official' live
release was something to behold and although this book will only chronicle
the purely audio release, the whole set was neatly packaged as three
complete live recordings. Two from the 'Wherever We May Roam' world tour
in 1992 and 1993 and one from the back end of the Damaged Justice tour
in 1989. A pleasing three-CD album took care of highlights from the Mexico
shows, while a VHS format (and later DVD) was utilised for the San Diego
and Seattle performances. The original box set came packaged as a mock
flight case, complete with a 72-page colour booklet, a 'scary guy' stencil and
even a faux snake pit concert pass for the real die-hard fans amongst us. A
comprehensive document of a tour like no other.

Disc One

'The Ecstasy of Gold/Enter Sandman' (7:28) (Ennio Morricone –
Hetfield/Ulrich/Hammett)
Originally released by Ennio Morricone as part of the 1966 soundtrack album
The Good, The Bad and The Ugly
Later recorded by the band in 2007 as part of the *We All Love Ennio
Morricone* tribute album, the original version of the 'Ecstasy of Gold' track
was utilised to open their shows as part of the 'Roam' tours. A fitting mood
and scene setter, it lends itself well as the soundtrack to our four heroes
taking up their positions on stage and blends seamlessly into the opening
bars of 'Sandman' here.

'Creeping Death' (7:28), **'Harvester of Sorrow'** (7:19), **'Welcome
Home (Sanitarium)'** (6:39), **'Sad but True'** (6:07), **'Of Wolf and Man'**
(6:22), **'The Unforgiven'** (6:48)

'Justice Medley' (9:38)

A cunning ploy to give the crowd a taste of some familiar old favourites, all tied up nicely in 'one big pile of shit' as coined by Hetfield. They kick things off with a rousing intro to 'Eye of the Beholder', but it doesn't last long and before we know it, we're straight into the thick of 'Blackened'. Then we're blasted into a quick tease of 'Frayed Ends of Sanity', which sets up an extended 'Justice' proper section. We finish with a typically breakneck section of 'Blackened' – the crowd lapping up every second.

'Solos' (18:49)

Solo spots in concerts are always a strange beast; they often tend to 'go on' a bit as happens here. At least proceedings kick off in a slightly surprising fashion here, however, with Newsted addressing the crowd and giving some richly deserved kudos to the roadcrew, before launching headlong into his 'My Friend of Misery' riff. After twiddling along in a Cliff-esque manner for a few minutes, Newsted is then casually joined by Kirk and the two of them explore some Zeppelin for a while before Kirk takes centre stage from 12:42.

Disc Two

'Through the Never' (3:47), **'For Whom the Bell Tolls'** (5:48), **'Fade to Black'** (7:12), **'Master of Puppets'** (4:35), **'Seek & Destroy'** (18:08), **'Whiplash'** (5:34)

Disc Three

'Nothing Else Matters' (6:22), **'Wherever I May Roam'** (6:33)

'Am I Evil?' (5:42) (Harris/Tatler)

Originally released by Diamond Head on the *Lightning to the Nations* album, 1980 Strangely omitted from that 'Garage Days' covers release a few years back (although they had previously recorded it and it will raise its ugly head again soon), its inclusion here is a knowing nod to our heroes' heroes.

Things start off pretty loose here – we're at the end of a long night of playing after all – and after the extended faithful intro, the band jam a little of Deep Purple's 'Smoke on the Water' and a little teaser of 'Enter Sandman'. It's not long before Kirk launches headlong into the introductory guitar solo part just before the main 'Am I Evil?' track kicks off. It's a faithful rendition, more of which will come later as part of another full covers/tribute album.

'Last Caress' (1:25), 'One' (10:27)

'So What/Battery' (10:05) (Exalt/Kulmer – Hetfield/Ulrich)

Originally released by Anti-Nowhere League as a B-side to the 'Streets of London' single, 1981

A short blues jam quickly morphs into teases of 'No Remorse' and 'Ride the Lightning', before a version of this shockingly disgusting track ('So What?') is performed for the masses.

A regular 'crowd pleaser' at Metallica gigs across the years, its original controversy is not hard to understand. The band recorded a version of their own for inclusion on the 'Unforgiven' vinyl and 'Sad but True' CD single releases and it will also appear on that previously mentioned second covers/tribute in a few years' time.

'The Four Horsemen' (6:08), 'Motorbreath' (3:14)

'Stone Cold Crazy' (5:32) (Mercury/May/Taylor/Deacon)
Originally released by Queen on the *Sheer Heart Attack* album, 1974
With incredible, relentless end-of-show energy, the band go out with a bang here, covering this classic Queen rock track.

Hetfield had already performed a version of this alongside Brian May, Roger Taylor, John Deacon (from Queen) and Tony Iommi (Black Sabbath) at the 1992 Freddie Mercury Tribute Concert. He adds his own twist to the song by adding a few expletives to the last verse. Metallica's own recorded rendition, released as a B-side to 'Enter Sandman', also appears on the 1990 compilation album *Elektra's 40th Anniversary*, and once again will feature on that upcoming covers/tribute album of their own.

At the end of this version, Hetfield, Kirk and Ulrich all thank the crowd, with Lars also informing the throng that the evening's performance has been recorded for none other than this – the band's first full-length live album. The Mexican crowd then sing us out gleefully to fade. Happy punters with many a memory made.

Load (1996)

Personnel:

Kirk Hammett: guitar
James Hetfield: guitar, vocals
Jason Newsted: bass
Lars Ulrich: drums
Recorded at: The Plant Studios, Sausalito, California between May 1995 and February 1996
Producer: Bob Rock with Hetfield and Ulrich
Release date: 4 June 1996
Chart placings: US: 1, UK: 1
Label: Elektra (US), Vertigo (UK)

With the Roam tour finally grinding to a well-earned halt at the Werchterpark in Belgium on 4 July 1993 and *Live Shit* keeping the record shelves stocked with new-ish material for the rest of the year, a break of some sort was needed to help the band take stock of the rollercoaster past couple of years and recharge their much-depleted batteries.

It didn't take long for the call of the crowd to return, however, and they were back out on the road as part of a series of 1994 'Summer Shit' shows running from 30 May to 21 August across Canada and the States, alongside acts including Danzig and Suicidal Tendencies. With new material urgently required, the dawn of a new year saw backs firmly to the drawing boards and in the writing room to see what post-*Black Album* Metallica would sound like.

The majority of 1995 was therefore spent crafting new fare, with only five live dates scheduled in total – most of which were imaginatively titled 'Escape From The Studio '95'.

The band saw out the year appearing as 'surprise' support act 'The Lemmys' at the Motorhead singer's 50th birthday celebrations at the Whiskey A Go Go in West Hollywood, California on 14 December. They played a set entirely made up of Motorhead numbers, including 'Overkill', 'Damage Case', 'Stone Dead Forever' and 'Too Late Too Late' - versions of which would later end up as B-sides to the new album's 'Hero of the Day' single releases in September 1996, after being recorded 'live' in the studio as part of the main sessions.

So five years on from 'that' album - what do we have? Well, it's the same line-up and producer, at least, but this time it's a slightly different sound (again) – a different band almost. There's no 'Master of Puppets' or lightning being ridden anymore. They seem to have settled on a new kind of style – less thrash, more solid rock.

It also appears that their recent experience of chart success has left a rather pleasant taste in their mouths as 'Until It Sleeps' (track four) is awakened and the commercialism continues with both 'King Nothing' (track five) and the aforementioned 'Hero of the Day' (track six) – compact, yet fully formed chunks of hard rock.

Side two (or three?) just doesn't seem to have quite the same immediate impact, though. 'Cure' (track eight) is just OK. The best thing about 'Poor Twisted Me' (track nine) is its hauntingly incessant riff which seems to bury deep into your subconscious and 'Wasting My Hate' (track ten) is just 'standard' fare.

'Mama Said' (track 11) is the best thing since a slice of the '2 X 4' (track two) you get bludgeoned with earlier in the album. Three things strike me about this track. Firstly, Hetfield's wonderfully double-tracked vocals in the chorus really bring the 'never I ask of you' part to life and secondly, Lars' playing is exactly as it should be – soft and delicate – particularly on the cymbals at the very end. Yes, I did just say 'soft and delicate'. The third is the cool country twang of the guitars.

'Outlaw Torn' (track 14) saves the best till last; nine minutes of heavy heaven. Its brilliance starts right from the fade-in intro and doesn't stop until the fade-out finish. Excellent lyrics and vocals, along with superb drum and bass playing.

So although black is definitely not 'back' in this case, progression is certainly made and with Bob Rock at the production helm once again, the 14 tracks which eventually emerged from the *Load* sessions certainly build on the power and assuredness of the previous studio release. There's also a return to more of a progressive nature, with three of the songs running at over six minutes. The foundations laid in the song structures found on the *Justice* album become firmer this time out. The crisp production also remains, but there's an edgier feel to proceedings, making it just slightly less radio-friendly overall.

The new direction was troubling some corners of the band, however, as Hetfield stated:

> There are some great, great songs on there, but my opinion is that all of the imagery and stuff like that was not necessary. And the amount of songs that were written ... diluted the potency of the poison of Metallica.

The album's artwork breaks slightly new ground, too, with a CD booklet of 30 pages depicting the band in various studio and city locations – thanks to Anton Corbijn's edgy photography – alongside selected lyrics from each song in turn. The minimalistic front cover features Andres Serrano's fiery design, with a new, simple black and white band logo.

On the back cover, all four band members are sat around a table, Hetfield and Kirk with cigars in hand. The CD inlay tray and CD itself also feature the Metallica ninja star design (four Ms) for the first time. In true new album launch gimmick mode, the band planned a series of appearances performing on the back of a truck in the car parks of various Tower Records stores across California. Unfortunately, only two of the planned three shows actually took place (San Jose and Sacramento), as the San Francisco authorities shut down their city's planned performance before a single note could be played. Too much hell for leather, perhaps, or just a case of civic responsibility? Let's allow the record to speak for itself.

'Ain't My Bitch' (5:04)

With a shedload of angst and power, the album comes bursting into life in a maelstrom of drums and guitar. In a similar vein to 'Holier Than Thou' from the *Black Album*, had it not been for the slightly 'radio unfriendly' title, this would most probably have been a good bet for the lead single. Hit aside, it's a firm statement of intent after almost five years of studio silence:

Headstrong,
What's wrong?
I've already heard this song before, you arrived,
But now it's time to kiss your ass goodbye.

In other words, 'tough shit if you don't like this new sound – this is *us*'.

The fury of the guitars under the 'so useless' lyric seems to confirm this sentiment. This is pure hard rock – it sounds tight and exciting, and it doesn't hold back. Hetfield's emphasis on the 'bitches' of the choruses are played with real aggression; in fact, he sounds like he's having the time of his life, particularly at 2:40 ahead of the guitar solo: 'outta my way!'

It all comes stuttering to a halt before a final reprise of the main riff at 4:55. A strong, confident start.

'2 X 4' (5:28) (Hetfield/Ulrich/Hammett)

Lars' presence is stamped all over this right from the outset with that impressive run around the snare and toms. The drum sound is exquisite on this album, building on from the compact sound of the *Black Album*. Here it's bolder and brighter than ever before, a real click to the snare drum in particular.

With a swagger and a swing, the main riff lifts this track into orbit, with Lars driving the song throughout and returning at the end of the chorus and verse intros with his kit runs. The one at 3:16 slows things down to a halftime beat with a suitable Kirk solo, before the drums rise up again to take us into the final bridge/chorus section.

Lyrically, it really packs some punch and, coming after the previous track's 'f*ck you' ethos, the intention is clear: 'I'm gonna make you, shake you, take you. I'm gonna be the one who breaks you'. Bit violent, lads!

What really brings this track to life, however, is the way Hetfield's vocal melody sits perfectly on top of the guitars, particularly in the verses – most notably the 'put the screws to you' sections. The timing is excellent, adding a real groove and feel to the composition.

'The House Jack Built' (6:39) (Hetfield/Ulrich/Hammett)

The first of those three six-minute-plus epics begins with a lazy, slow-burning riff – there is something brewing here. At 48 seconds, an evil riff is then summoned as the track starts to go through its gears. Hetfield plays the vocal part so well; it's almost like a dark show tune, a tale of an abused life and an all-consumed anti-hero. He acts out the lyrics in an impressive, expressive manner, no more so than at the 'is that you there, or just another demon that I meet?' section at 2:52.

The harrowing solo from 3:46 extends to 4:38 and we hear the demon writhing inside – unshakeable. We come to a close with two rounds of the chorus before Hetfield 'twist(s) away' again during the outro, confirming he'll never be free.

'Until it Sleeps' (4:30)

Finally, we get a single – the first one from this set. Released just prior to the album, two weeks before to be precise, it hit No.10 and No.5 in the US and UK charts, respectively.

Like an extension of the previous track's lyrical sentiment – the demon still has a tight grip – the subject matter is not the most universally accessible. Lars' deft snare drum flams on the verses set this song apart from others on the album, however. It shows the diversity and flexibility of his playing – he's never been just a hit and hoper and here he underlines it for us. An understated Kirk solo from 2:58 perfectly fits the bill and as the song draws to a close, that deft snare drum playing shifts gear for two rounds of full fills, before we crawl back into the shadowy darkness to the end.

'King Nothing' (5:28) (Hetfield/Ulrich/Hammett)

Here comes single two – albeit the final release from the album and one that barely troubled the charts (US: 90). A steady Newsted bass run introduces the main riff here and it's pretty much standard rock and roll fare throughout – this would not have sounded out of place on the *Black Album*.

There is a nice harmonic riff over the bridge section, which emphasises the vocal melody well and Hetfield spits out the track's title with real venom – 'where's your crown, King Nothing?!'

The start of Kirk's solo mirrors the bridge melody again and from 3:55, we get a spoken word section which builds effectively to the final chorus. A surprising, almost mumbled 'off to Never, Never Land' rings out at the end. Perhaps a nod to the fact these chart kings have fallen slightly from grace these days?

'Hero of the Day' (4:22) (Hetfield/Ulrich/Hammett)

We wait three tracks and then three singles come all at once – this the second to be released from the album – number 60 in the US and number 17 in the UK.

An almost lullaby-esque intro gently heralds the start of this track, a muffled effect on Hetfield's vocal masking the first recurring 'mama they try and break me' line.

If ever a track screamed 'trying to be a hit single' it must be this one. You can hear them trying their hardest, too, until we get to 2:16 and the full force is released once more. It's as if they've thrown the songbook out of the window – tired of trying to please the masses again – and just gone all out metal on our asses. It works, too and whips the song into a frenzy and into a pleasing, more commercial-sounding Kirk solo from 2:39.

After a final chorus, the frenzied mesh of guitars and pounding drums return to a crescendo. 'Mama they try ...'

'Bleeding Me' (8:18) (Hetfield/Ulrich/Hammett)

Another lazy, bass-heavy introductory riff leads in a bright, clean guitar sound before Hetfield croons his way through the verse sections of this eight-minute-plus opus. It's another slow burner, and Kirk's rather understated and, again, clean-sounding solo, sandwiched between two choruses, acts as a neat lynchpin to the song's turn at 4:48.

Here, a new riff kicks in, which drives Hetfield insanely to the final chorus: 'I am the beast that feeds the feast', he growls. Kirk then sees us safely home with a second solo over a double-time speed section and there's a return to the opening riff to bring what would have been, if time and appetite had allowed, a calming end to side one of the record.

This track is the sole example of an attempt at the 'two in one song' trick on this album that was glaringly absent on the previous one yet featured prominently on *Ride the Lightning, Puppetz* and *Justice*.

'Cure' (4:54)

After such a strong seven-track run, the quality of the songs dips a little from this point, although there are glints of diamonds in the rough.

Lars kicks things off this time, driving the main riff with precision and accuracy over an introductory spoken word opening: 'The man takes another bullet, he keeps them all within. He must seek, no matter how it hurts. So don't fool again'.

The pre-chorus run on the toms dovetails neatly with the guitars as Hetfield launches in full force – 'betting on the cure, it must get better than this.' The way he snarls 'precious cure' in the end sections is perfectly done too. As are his shouts of 'I do believe!' as he takes us screaming to the end.

'Poor Twisted Me' (4:00)

A clever echo/delay on the main guitar riff – the real hook of the song – announces the start of this track, which burrows deep into the consciousness, with the vocal melody effectively filling the gaps it leaves in the verse sections. There's a cool compressed effect on Hetfield's vocal and his prolonged hang on the 'me' in the choruses, only further underlines the agony his latest character feels – 'oh woe is me, such a burden to be, oh poor twisted me'. A familiar theme of internal loathing and self-recrimination lingers on this album and this particular track – not a happy place to be, it seems – but one they'd name their upcoming tour after. The effect compressed on the guitar at the start suddenly ceases in the second half of the solo, before we're brought to an emphatic end after a final, Hetfield-wailed chorus.

'Wasting My Hate' (3:57) (Hetfield/Ulrich/Hammett)

A jaunty, almost jolly little guitar riff sets the tone here – with Hetfield's distant vocal – until the drums and guitars come crashing in at 28 seconds to make it business as usual again. It's akin to the start of 'Hero of the Day' from earlier in the album, but the main, driving riff here keeps the energy up for almost the full four minutes.

Lars utilises the snare to great effect to bridge from verse to chorus, ensuring this track, the shortest on the album, motors along with pace until its abrupt end.

'Mama Said' (5:19)

The acoustic country twang to this track is a welcome departure from the ferocity we've been subjected to so far. A chance to regroup, draw breath and take a little step back for a few minutes.

A pained tale of a mother and son's struggle with their tumultuous relationship over the years, unfortunately never to be fully repaired, is told with true emotion and impact here, most notably in the final verse, bridge and chorus sections:

Mama, now I'm coming home, I'm not all you wished of me. A mother's love for her son, unspoken help me be. I took your love for granted and all the things you said to me. I need your arms to mother me, but cold stone's all I see.

The country-esque slide guitar passages at the start of the bridge sections are played with real emotion and Hetfield's impeccable double-tracked vocal hits the feels right where they hurt in the latter stages of the choruses. Lars' light touch, especially the tinkles on the cymbals throughout this song, show further proof of the versatility his playing can reach at times too.

The album's fourth single release – reaching a wholly acceptable number 19 in the UK charts – disappointingly failed to chart at all back home.

'Thorn Within' (5:51) (Hetfield/Ulrich/Hammett)

It takes a little while for this brooding monster to stir into life – 1:16 before the vocal kicks in. The energy soon arrives, however, by way of the chorus and that ferocious, recurring 'Hero of the Day' whip at 2:12: 'I am the secret, I am the sin. I am the guilty/I am the thorn within'. Further evidence of self-recrimination.

They're not letting us settle at all here – no sooner have we taken a short rest with 'mama', they're then back knocking us into shape and reminding us of their true cause – a shed 'load' of heartache.

'Ronnie' (5:17)
Another infectious, brain-drilling riff announces the penultimate track. Its loop from 44 seconds in makes it a difficult one to shake amongst an album of killer hooks and devices.

The vocal melody cleverly mirrors the guitar refrain in the chorus, sounding initially like an all-out wild west-themed tale – guns-a-totin' and necks-a-hanging. An outlaw to be caught and punished: 'story starts, quiet town. Small-town boy, big-time frown. Never talks, never plays. Different path, lost his way'.

It's only at 3:29, during a spoken word section, that Hetfield reveals the song's true theme: 'All the green things died when Ronnie moved to this place/now we all know why the children called him Ronnie frown, when he pulled that gun from his pocket, they all fall down'. An examination of the troubled gun law and horribly re-occurring mass shootings that were all too prevalent in the mid-90s in the States, it seems.

The real outlaw is fast approaching, though and he's up next ...

'The Outlaw Torn' (9:53)
...lumbering into earshot out of fade and tapping us on the shoulder like a familiar friend. A marathon, not sprint, this album may have been, but here we have a track that seems to encompass everything about what post-*Black Album* Metallica are really about.

There is so much to enjoy, not least Newsted's careful walking verse basslines, but the real trick is the repeated guitar licks which echo out on top of it throughout the song. They add a new air of intrigue and mystery, all sounding different and complementing the track's macabre nature so well – prog metal rock if you like!

Lars pounds the snare and toms in perfect time with the guitars in the chorus, as if egging on Hetfield to deliver his vocal goods and then from 5:22, as the track settles and Newsted adopts a chilled-out, almost spacey effect on bass, the guitar solo builds up until it screams out and wails like a cursed child at 6:43. It sounds like it could go on forever and probably should have, but from 8:03, as a new riff chimes in, it heralds the beginning of the end and Lars double-times the drum pattern to fade.

My favourite track on the album and also in my all-time top three Metallica tracks – simply down to Kirk's wonderful lead guitar playing. 'Jump in the Fire' from *Kill 'Em All* is my number one (in case you can't

57

remember), with the *Black Album*'s 'Wherever I May Roam' at number two –
just for the records...

All in all, I think it would have been a much stronger ten track album –
omitting 'Cure', 'Wasting My Hate', 'Thorn Within' and 'Ronnie' - which often
feel like they're making up the numbers – B-sides at best most probably. Oh
well, fancy a *Reload*?

Reload (1997)

Personnel:
Kirk Hammett: guitars
James Hetfield: guitars, vocals
Jason Newsted: bass
Lars Ulrich: drums
Jim McGillveray: percussion
David Miles: hurdy-gurdy
Bernado Bigalli: violin
Marianne Faithfull: vocals
Recorded at: The Plant Studios, Sausalito, California between May 1995 and
February 1996 and between July and October 1997
Producer: Bob Rock with Hetfield and Ulrich
Release date: 18 November 1997
Chart placings: US: 4, UK: 1
Label: Elektra (US), Vertigo (UK)

Like an imperfect bookend, just shy of eighteen months since their previous effort was 'unloaded', we get a second bite of the cherry and another thirteen new Bob Rocked tracks to enjoy – it's almost as if they planned it this way.

After *Load*'s June 1996 release, Lollapalooza dates across Canada and the States busied Metallica's schedule up to 4 August, until the ironic 'Poor Touring Me' tour kicked off in Vienna, Austria on 6 September, running until 28 May the following year.

So fruitful had the *Load* sessions been, that in addition to another Plant Studios stint in the second half of 1997, another thirteen tracks were also written and recorded, meaning there was enough material for an entire new album. Not quite the *Use Your Illusion* concept that Guns N' Roses had marketed so cleverly in the early 1990s, but a neat 'part two' package, nonetheless, cunningly coined *Reload* for clarity.

'Fuel' (track one) is definitely up a notch from the start of the previous collection – right from Hetfield's lambasting intro, through to some great drums on the chorus and Kirk's piercing solo and riffaging rumbling to the end.

'Memory Remains' (track two) retains a quality start – with a brilliant crowd-pleasing chorus and some incredibly haunting female cameo backing vocals.

Later, the familiar swell of 'The Unforgiven' introduces us to part two, but that's pretty much the only familiar thing on offer. They don't try to mess with the *Black Album* original at all (intro apart). Even the lyrics in its chorus don't really hark back to the past. A stand-alone track with its own merit.

And strategically placed in the same track position as 'Mama Said' on *Load* - 'Low Man's Lyric' (track 11) is another nice mood changer surrounding a few more 'forgettable' tunes in my opinion, as the album fully unfolds – more filler than killer this time I'm afraid and overall as a concept, I much prefer my first 'load' to the refill.

Nonetheless, to help promote this new batch of material, the 'Blitzkrieg '97' tour ran from 22 August at Belgium's Pukkelpop Festival into late November, encompassing a number of special/one-off appearances including *Top of the Pops* and radio shows in the UK.

There's no doubt that most of these new songs stemmed from the original *Load* recording sessions – you can hear it clear as day. Bob Rock's 'live take' ethos is evident again; this could have been a double album and for all intents and purposes, it is – just with a fifteen-month release gap. As Lars summed up the project:

> I think a lot of people think it's just the scraps, but it's not. I have to sit there and convince myself that I've written 27 songs that are equally good. If number seventeen wasn't good enough, I'd throw it away ... we normally stop at twelve when we write albums, but we knew that we wanted to develop all 27 ... that they were all good enough.

The cover artwork is much the same, too – same new black and white band logo and same *Load* font – this time with a hastily scrawled *RE* in front of the *Load*. Andres Serrano supplies the main front image again, this time the imaginatively titled 'Piss & Blood' – best not to ask. Anton Corbijn returns as the photographer for the CD liner notes, featuring solely live-action 'show' shots alongside lyric excerpts as per *Load*. The CD inlay tray and physical CD again feature the Metallica ninja star design. The back cover features suitably ferocious 'live show' headshots of each member.

'Fuel' (4:29) (Hetfield/Ulrich/Hammett)
Hetfield barks the chorus lyrics at us - 'gimme fuel, gimme fire, gimme that which I desire' - and the main riff, panned to the right at first, kicks off the new album full throttle. There's no let up as we race through verse one before Lars works the snare, toms and kick during the bridge section. It's full speed ahead when the half-time rhythm kicks in again at 1:28 and we drop a gear, cruising past whoever's in front of us as we accelerate on down the highway, leaving everyone and everything in our wake. A fantastic driving song.

Lyrically, it goes nowhere but the highway - 'one hundred plus, through black and white. Warhorse, warhead, f*ck 'em, man, white-knuckle tight'. Hetfield is absolutely in his element here, guzzling the gasoline by the second.

Kirk's excellent solo then takes us careering into the final bend and Hetfield summons his last ounce of energy as we screech to a halt.

The third and final single release from the album. A UK number 31, not charting in the US – shame.

'The Memory Remains' (4:39)
We draw breath just for a second before Hetfield is back again, bold as brass, his vocal melody sitting right on top of the crunching guitar riff. There's a

snake-like feel to the verses here – a theme that will continue to resurface throughout the album – and Lars' punchy snare drum drives this anthem all the way through. When Hetfield holds onto that 'memory' chorus lyric, you can hear the stadium crowd singing it too. But here's the trick...

The excellent guest vocalist – a first for Metallica on record – doesn't pipe up until the 1:58 mark. They keep us waiting and boy, does it pay off. Marianne Faithfull's haunting, timeless melody steals the show and lifts the song to the next level. Hetfield then comes bruising back in brilliantly, emphasising the 'fade to black' lyric with emphatic clarity and great diction. Kirk lets his guitar ring out at the start of his solo and then his harmonics over Marianne's returning vocal, along with Lars' restrained playing, bring us to an unsettling climax as the 'little tin goddess' 'faithfully' disappears into obscurity once again: 'Say yes, at least say hello'. Chilling stuff.

The lead single – released a week before the album. Hitting number 28 in the US and a more respectable number 13 in the UK and my favourite track on the album, mainly due to the haunting nature of its finale.

N.B. CDS two featured a version of 'The Outlaw Torn' subtitled: (Unencumbered by Manufacturing Restrictions Version). It seemed that 9:53 wasn't quite long enough for the band and had to be cut slightly to fit on a standard CD running format.

'Devil's Dance' (5:18)

A groovy Newsted stomp begins things before suddenly a guitar – again panned to the right – growls into life. After a few moments, an incredibly hooky guitar line builds. It repeats and gains momentum until Hetfield lets us know he's there 'too'.

The guitars in the chorus sound like sledgehammers and then there's a snappy 'let's dance' vocal. A snake is literally mentioned this time – 'tempting, that bite to take' – and Kirk's solo at 3:15 sounds like it's coiling round and around, squeezing the very lives out of us. There's a real devil troubling our souls at 4:25 as well. Oh, and it's on my Halloween playlist again, of course: 'It's nice to see you here. Ha ha ...!'

This should have been a single, in my opinion.

'The Unforgiven II' (6:36) (Hetfield/Ulrich/Hammett)

The sequel. The final act? Or is it? We'll see ...

But as that hornpipe swells again, this time there are no acoustic guitars, just a clean, country, 'Mama Said'-style twang after the suffocating, familiar wall of sound. Hetfield's soulful tone returns and the clever reprise of the part one lyric in the chorus reminds us all of where we really are – 'what I've felt, what I've known, turn the pages, turn the stone'.

After Kirk's solo and the breakdown, Lars attacks the drums in true 'Unforgiven' fashion to guide us inevitably towards the end. And as Hetfield wilfully mourns 'never free, never me' once more, we understand that this new character is forever destined to be unforgiven too.

The second single release from the album, faring slightly less favourably than its predecessor. A confusing number 59 in the US but a UK number 15 again.

'Better Than You' (5:21)

After a sentimental blast from a recent past, we regroup to a looping guitar effect which leads to Lars building steadily on the toms around the main riff. As Hetfield growls the title over the chorus, that devil reappears, mimicking the vocal in a suitably disturbed nature.

This is Metallica at their heaviest best and they play on it well in the latter section, leading out with a second solo and finishing strongly with a looping chorus, ending with a return to the introductory guitar effect to fade.

'Slither' (5:13) (Hetfield/Ulrich/Hammett)

The snake writhes again, right from the start here – 'don't go looking for (them), you might find them' – before the crunching guitars introduce the main riff. Hetfield plays the part strongly once more, particularly in the 'see you crawlin'' section, with the effect on the vocals adding to the serpentine nature of the song. Lars feeds off the back end of Kirk's solo as if taunting him to give us a bit more and there's a rehearsal room, jam feel to the end.

'Carpe Diem Baby' (6:12) (Hetfield/Ulrich/Hammett)

A strong main riff courses through the intro and Lars builds the momentum from the verse as the chorus approaches, allowing Hetfield to really let loose. He acts out the role brilliantly, the lines fairly tripping off his tongue – 'come squeeze and suck the day, come carpe diem baby'.

At 4:04, during the instrumental section, the guitars squeal against the beat of the drums as the rhythm of the track takes hold. Hetfield drops it all down a little before we approach the end – 'live, win. Dare, fail. Eat dirt, bite the nail' – as the main riff batters us to a finish.

They could have 'seized the day' with this, if you'll pardon the pun, as it's another strong single contender for me. An opportunity ironically missed.

'Bad Seed' (4:05) (Hetfield/Ulrich/Hammett)

It's from hereon in (tracks 11 and 13 apart), rather like the *Load* before it, that the album starts to falter, becoming ploddy and a little laboured, in my opinion.

With a spluttered cough, Hetfield spits this track into life. The spoken word, almost ringmaster-like bridge sections, lends a real circus feel to proceedings: 'ladies and gentlemen, step right up and see the man who told the truth'. But Lars fancies stealing the show as he brings in the full force of the double kick pedal from 2:10.

He lets Kirk take over for a solo and then Hetfield regains centre stage, relishing his vocal duties once more. Another cough and a splutter and we're out.

The shortest track on the album and one that Metallica have not yet played live.

'Where the Wild Things Are' (6:52) (Hetfield/Ulrich/Newsted)

A Newsted writing credit! The only one from across the entire *Load/Reload* sessions. Tells another little tale, perhaps? We'll have to wait and find out.

In the meantime, his presence is stamped all over this track. Firstly, in the haunting introductory guitar melody and secondly, in the thunderous basslines of the verses – the speakers almost burst at the seams if the volume's (always) high enough – it's ear-bleedingly good. As is Kirk's sinister 'wah-wah' solo from 3:39. Lars brings in some crisp-sounding military drumming at 4:26 before Hetfield conjures that snakelike charm again, twisting his vocal as we head into the final chorus.

'Prince Charming' (6:04)

'Hey, Mom! Look, it's me!' They're here in all their twisted glory.

And although the intro fools us into thinking this might be another 'Memory Remains' slow burner, it soon bursts into life and all hell breaks loose. 'I'm the filthy one', teases Hetfield and he sounds like he is too. There's a real 'Four Horseman' feel to the melody of the bridge and after Hetfield boasts to Mom in the first chorus proper, Lars pummels the floor tom to introduce verse two. It sounds like they're having a good time on this track – probably for the first time across the entire *Load* sessions – like they're finally letting go.

Maybe the pressures of global fame had reached a pinnacle and they just thought, 'f*ck this' let's have some fun.

'Low Man's Lyric' (7:36)

Cunningly placed at track eleven, just like 'Mama Said' on the previous album – funny that – this acoustic-based number brings the level down again for a while. Just like on the previous album, too – doubly funny.

The lyrical content here is much darker, though; this 'low man' is very low – 'I can't bear to see, what I've let me be/bring this poor dog in from the rain, though he just wants right back out again'. This is heartbreaking, poignant stuff.

Lars' playing is spot on too – as is his drum sound – kick so soft, snare almost caressed by his sticks. And the hurdy-gurdy is just, well – hurdy-gurdy-ish. But it sits so perfectly in this song, as if nothing else could be there. The instrumental section from 3:37 is exceptional. It sounds like a piano playing the lead part, but it's not, it's guitars, of course. We end with that hurdy-gurdy playing out to everyone, anyone. Will that low man ever come out on top? Who knows?

'Attitude' (5:16)

Back with a mother-f*cking bang and don't we know it! It's absolute brute force again – 'attitude' bleeding from the speakers. Not so much gay abandon here as there was with 'Prince Charming' just before it, though – it feels like they're holding back on us a little. A bit like metal-by-numbers – a low point on the album? Not one to skip, but there's better company.

'Fixxxer' (8:15) (Hetfield/Ulrich/Hammett)

Again, like 'Low Man', this last epic tale is strategically placed just like 'Outlaw Torn' on the album before – as the final track – albeit track 13 this time and not track 14.

Another out-of-fade intro, with another looping guitar effect (like 'Better Than You'). Then Newsted and Lars – with help from the guitars – bleed this song into life. It's another pained lyric: 'Can you heal what father's done? Or fix this hole in a mother's son?' There's a bastard at work here, one we don't want to win.

From 4:14, there's another extended 'jam-like' instrumental section, unlike 'Outlaw Torn', which always seemed structured and secure. This feels like it could break loose at any moment, spiralling out of control, and it almost does until 5:34 when Newsted and Lars lock tight in unison, then bring it all up to a dramatic climax: 'Just when all seems fine and I'm pain-free, you jab another pin, jab another pin in me'. Father, you bastard.

As we come to the end, Lars double-times the tempo and Hetfield lets all that pent-up agony go – 'no more, no more, no more, no, no, no', he cries out.

Above: From left to right: Cliff, Lars and Hetfield, with Dave Mustaine, 1983. (*metallica.com*)

Below: A 'new' Metallica, 2003. From left to right: Trujillo, Kirk, Lars and Hetfield. (*metallica.com*)

Left: The 'Jump in the Fire' single cover – 'demons arise' – the first single. (*Megaforce/Music For Nations*)

Right: *Kill 'Em All* – that knock-out debut. (*Megaforce/Music For Nations*)

Left: *Ride the Lightning* – 'death in the air, strapped in the electric chair' – that not so difficult, as it turned out, second album. (*Megaforce/Music For Nations*)

Right: *Master of Puppets*: a turning point and Cliff Burton's last stand. Some way to go out – RIP. (*Elektra/Music For Nations*)

Left: *Garage Days Re-Revisited.* Healing and regrouping with an EP tribute to some of their heroes. (*Elektra/Vertigo*)

Right: *... And Justice For All.* Featuring 'one' of their biggest hits; shame the sound wasn't up to scratch. (*Elektra/Vertigo*)

Above: Cliff (left) and Hetfield, 1983. (*metallica.com*)

Below: Cliff at Donington, UK, 1985. (*metallica.com*)

Above: Thrash, not trash, 1986. From left to right: Cliff, Lars, Hetfield and Kirk. (*metallica.com*)

Below: In the studio, 1987. From left to right: Lars, Kirk, Newsted and Hetfield. (*metallica.com*)

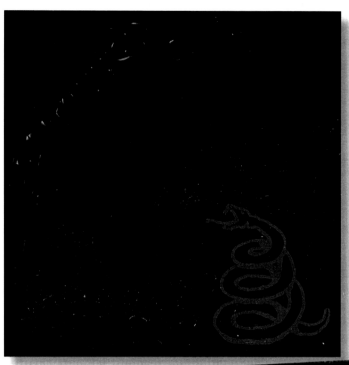

Left: The *Black Album* – the ultimate game changer. (*Elektra/Vertigo*)

Right: The 'Enter Sandman' single cover. The trademark tune – heavy metal brought to the masses. (*Elektra/Vertigo*)

ENTER SANDMAN

Right: *Live Shit: Binge & Purge.* A roaming document of a band at the peak of their powers. (*Elektra/Vertigo*)

Left: *Load.* Outlaws torn – a Metallica for the 90s. (*Elektra/Vertigo*)

Left: *Reload*. The
memory remained
– *Load* mark two.
(*Elektra/Vertigo*)

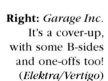

Right: *Garage Inc.*
It's a cover-up,
with some B-sides
and one-offs too!
(*Elektra/Vertigo*)

Right: *S&M.* Symphony and Metallica – what could possibly go wrong? (*Elektra/ Vertigo*)

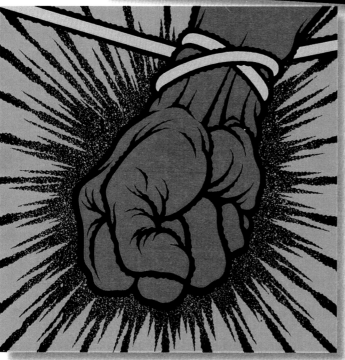

Left: *St. Anger.* Cover your ears and strap yourself in. (*Elektra/Vertigo*)

Left: Not 'Bohemian Rhapsody', 1991. Clockwise from top left: Newsted, Hetfield, Kirk and Lars. (*metallica.com*)

Right: Loads where else to roam, 1993. From left to right: Lars, Newsted (nice hair!), Hetfield and Kirk. (*metallica.com*)

Right: Get a 'load' of this lot, 1996. From left to right: Hetfield, Newsted, Lars and Kirk. (*metallica.com*)

Left: 'Garage InK', 1998. From left to right: Lars, Kirk, Hetfield and Newsted. (*metallica.com*)

Left: *Death Magnetic.* The end of the road that pulls us all in eventually: the 'white elephant in the room'. (*Warner Bros./Vertigo*)

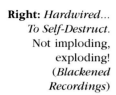

Right: *Hardwired... To Self-Destruct.* Not imploding, exploding! (*Blackened Recordings*)

Right: *S&M 2.* Symphony and Metallica: the reprise. (*Blackened Recordings*)

Left: *72 Seasons* – all in one day. A metal concept for the 21st century. (*Blackened Recordings*)

Left: *Through the Never.*
Metallica at the movies.
(*Blackened Recordings*)

Right: The Metallicats on
the cover of the 'Die, Die
My Darling' single, 1998.
From left to right: Kirk,
Hetfield, Newsted and Lars.
(*Blackened Recordings*)

Left: Download
2006 ticket. On
a sweaty day
in June, I was
privileged to hear
Puppetz in its
entirety for its
20th anniversary.
(*Barry Wood*)

Right: Download 2006. Kirk (left) and Hetfield. (*metallica.com*)

Left: Download from up in the air, 10 June 2023. (*metallica.com*)

Right: Bidding (another) fond farewell to the Download crowd on night two, 10 June 2023. (*metallica.com*)

Left: Milton Keynes, UK ticket, 1993 – do you remember the first time? My first Metallica concert. (*Barry Wood*)

Right: The *Madly in Anger With the World* tour, Earls Court, UK ticket, 2003 – they didn't play 'St. Anger' – doh! (*Barry Wood*)

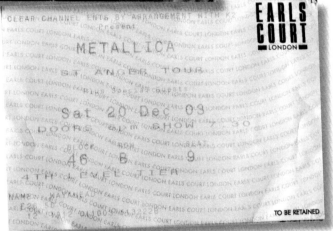

Above: Metallica in Manchester ticket, 2019 – my last attempt, for now. (*Barry Wood*)

Garage Inc. (1998)

Personnel:
Cliff Burton: bass (on the Garage Days Revisited '84 tracks)
Kirk Hammett: guitars
James Hetfield: guitars, vocals
Jason Newsted: bass
Lars Ulrich: drums
Recorded at: The Plant Studios, Sausalito, California in December 1995 and
September and October 1998, A&M and Conway, Los Angeles, California, 1987
(The $5.98 E.P. – Garage Days Re-Revisited), Sausalito, California, 1984 (Garage
Days Revisited '84), Los Angeles, California, 1988 ('Harvester of Sorrow' B-sides),
Berkeley, California, 1990 (track ten, disc two) and Los Angeles, California, 1991
('The Unforgiven' B-sides).
Producer: Somewhat produced by Bob Rock with Hetfield and Ulrich, not very
produced (The $5.98 E.P. – Garage Days Re-Revisited) and kind of produced (track
ten, disc two) by Metallica, roughly produced by Bob Rock with Hetfield and
Ulrich ('The Unforgiven' B-sides) and Mark Whitaker (Garage Days Revisited '84)
Release date: 24 November 1998
Chart placings: US: 29, UK: 2
Label: Elektra (US), Vertigo (UK)

Cover versions, as we've already seen with the *$5.98 E.P. – Garage Days Re-Revisited*, were a big part of Metallica's initial development, just like they are with most bands starting out on the road to world domination. Ever since their first show back in March 1982 at Radio City in Anaheim, California, they've often thrown in a sprinkling of covers – tributes to the artists that helped shape them and form their distinctive style and sound over the years. There's more than just a sprinkling here, however, their eighth studio album proper – a double set, with new and not-so-new recordings of their favourite tracks from their favourite bands.

Disc one features 11 new tracks, all but one of them laid down at the now familiar Plant Studios in Sausalito, where the *Load*s had been so lovingly crafted. Disc two holds an eclectic mix of old favourites, including the full *$5.98 E.P. – Garage Days Re-Revisited*, along with various B-sides, 'one-offs' and special editions.

What might have been seen as a bit of a cop-out, therefore – a mere 'covers' album at first glance – on closer inspection and multiple listens, this album allows a deeper glimpse into the kind of styles and influences the band soaked up back in the day.

It's also an excellent addition for those fans who may not have rushed out to buy every single thing Metallica has ever released – with the collection of odds and sods and rarities liable to keep many a Metalli-nut happy. The inclusion of the Newsted debut 'Garage Days Re-Revisited' is a nice touch, as is the 'Motorheadache' EP – a good homage to the old stalwarts – which was recorded during the original Load sessions back in 1995. All in all, a cool collection of songs for fans. Another nice stop-gap after the previous two albums. Probably not one of the 'go-to' albums for many fans, but good to dip into every now and again for something a bit different.

After 'Blitzkrieg' came to an end at the end of 1997, Metallica kicked off their live show stretch in 1998 with the 'Poor ReTouring Me' tour in Newcastle, Australia, on 2 April. This ran around the world until 13 September in San Diego, after which they promptly cancelled and rescheduled the rest of the dates so they could work on the new cover tracks for the album.

Sounding extremely *Load* like throughout, *Garage Inc.* yet again has the Bob Rock sonic imprint stamped all over it. There's even more of a live feel to this release, however, akin to 1987's *$5.98 E.P.* – fun being had and a real sense of letting off steam from the constant touring schedule shining through. The album cover artwork is a real departure this time. No abstract Andres Serrano designs anymore. Here we have a more tongue-in-cheek approach, the front cover depicting the band members as suitably oiled-up grease monkeys outside a yes, you've guessed it, car garage. The back cover features the image from the original *$5.98 E.P.* release, but with current band headshots clumsily taped over the old ones.

Inside the CD inlay, Anton Corbijn's photography peppers an extensive 32-page booklet of historical studio images, alongside some excellent and detailed liner notes from *Rolling Stone*'s own David Fricke. The back cover of the CD features a highly amusing shot of the band decked out in full evening attire pictured as bar crooners 'The Metallicats' – 'appearing nightly, covering all your favourites', reads the heading. More chaos than crooning this release creates, however.

Disc One
New Recordings '98
'Free Speech for the Dumb' (2:35) (Morris/Wainwright/Molaney/Roberts)
Originally released by Discharge on the *Hear Nothing See Nothing Say Nothing* album, 1982
Back in those pre-'Garage Days Re-Revisited', Discharge featured heavily on Metallica's playlists. This track is a ferocious start to this new set – drums and guitars pummelling the listener into submission early doors. The irony of the title is not lost either, being the only lyric in the song. Hetfield adds an extra expletive for good measure in what is a very faithful rendition of a right raucous classic.

'It's Electric' (3:33) (Tatler/Harris)
Originally released by Diamond Head on the *Lightning to the Nations* album, 1980
If there is one NWOBHM band that Metallica soaked in more during the early days, you'll be hard-pressed to find them. The Birmingham-based (UK)

foursome, formed in 1977, were a clear passion, especially for Lars, who actually got to know and share a room with singer Sean Harris and guitarist Brian Tatler during a pilgrimage to London in the summer of 1981 to see them in all their metal glory. A glory that shines out in this track – more cheese than speed – 'I'm gonna be a rock and roll star, gonna groove from night to day'. There's little of the 'evil' expressed in the previous (*Live Shit*) cover we've recently considered, but they certainly bring the groove to this version, and you can clearly hear the love.

'Sabbra Cadabra' (6:20) (Black Sabbath)
Originally released by Black Sabbath on the *Sabbath Bloody Sabbath* album, 1973
Not an obvious choice to cover on paper, perhaps, but as soon as that killer riff kicks in, it's not hard to hear why they picked this particular tune. The energy is sustained throughout, and they stamp their own take on things by omitting the original's 'spacey' middle section, choosing instead to conjure a short blast of Sabbath's 'A National Acrobat', also from the *Sabbath Bloody Sabbath* album. Bloody marvellous.

'Turn the Page' (6:06) (Seger)
Originally released by Bob Seger on the *Back In '72* album, 1973
A lonesome rhythm guitar rings out to usher in this mournful tale of life on the road – something Metallica know all too well about. This is not a story about hotel trashing, drug-fuelled debauchery or bed(fan) hopping, though – it's one of the grit and determination of an existence 'up on the stage'. The blood, sweat and tears. The playing to that one man and his dog audience in back-room bars again. The days of obscurity that must be lived, in order for the next level to be achieved.

It's perfectly interpreted by Hetfield, his crooning vocal emulating Seger's original performance in a fitting tribute. As the dynamics ebb and flow, however, the band express their power in good measure to lift this version a little higher in places than its 1973 predecessor. Kirk's excellent lead guitar playing – particularly the reoccurring refrain that threads through the entire track – is played with real soul, more so than the saxophone that was used on the original.

Chosen as the lead single from the album – released on 16 November 1998, it spectacularly failed to chart on either side of the Atlantic.

'Die, Die My Darling' (2:26) (Danzig)
Originally released by The Misfits as a 1984 single
The Misfits were a band that former bassist Cliff Burton ruthlessly forced on his bandmates in Metallica's early days, battering their eardrums on a constant loop, driving to gigs and rehearsals as they cut their teeth – until the sounds gradually seeped into their collective subconsciousness. It's fitting then that this murderous tribute is included here, a knowing nod to both. The third and

67

final single lifted from this set. Released on 7 June 1999 and again it failed to chart on either side of the pond.

'Loverman' (7:52) (Cave)
Originally released by Nick Cave and the Bad Seeds on the *Let Love In* album, 1994

Now and again, a cover version takes on a life of its own, often being comparable to the original – sometimes better than. Think Hendrix's 'Watchtower' or Guns N' Roses' 'Live and Let Die' and arguably their rendition of 'Knockin' On Heaven's Door' from *Use Your Illusion II* as well. This brooding, lumbering take on Nick Cave's disturbing ballad falls in that category for me – apologies to all Cave fans.

Dynamically again, it's far superior to the original, Hetfield holding the breaks in the chorus passages just long enough for the listener's anticipation to peak. And when the full band is unleashed, it's with an evil might and fury to match no other, making it my favourite cover on the album.

Cave's original, although equally unsettling in its vocal delivery, lacks this powerful threat, meandering along with less bite and far less menace. Just my opinion, but listen to this version, then the original back-to-back and see what you think.

'Mercyful Fate' (featuring 'Satan's Fall', 'Curse of the Pharaohs', 'A Corpse Without Soul', 'Into The Coven' and 'Evil') (11:10) (Shermann/ Diamond)
Originally released by Mercyful Fate on the *Mercyful Fate* EP, 1982 and the Melissa album, 1983

Medleys have been dabbled in briefly before (the *Justice* mash-up on *Live Shit* and 'Kill/Ride Medley', which was released as part of the 'Until It Sleeps' single, recorded at the Monsters of Rock festival, Castle Donington, UK, on 26 August 1995) but neither were quite as ambitious or lengthy as this. Formed at the same time as Metallica, Mercyful Fate hailed from Denmark and carried more than a few satanical tendencies. This medley screeches along at quite a pace, similar to the original band's own lead singer – the enigmatic King Diamond.

'Astronomy' (6:37) (Pearlman/A. Bouchard/J. Bouchard)
Originally released by Blue Öyster Cult on the *Secret Treaties* album, 1974

If Diamond Head, Misfits and Discharge were all staples of early Metallica life, Blue Öyster Cult were a sure-fire favourite of Newsted, who grew up with their progressive trend of dark metal in his concert-going teenage years. The sombre mood of the original is captured authentically in this version, Hetfield mimicking the high-pitched vocal phrasing well. Lars' kick drum beats deftly in the intro section before the main guitar refrain kicks in a 1:40. Hetfield then leads the band in unison, chanting 'hey!' above a familiar barrage of metal. Newsted's fondness for this track is noticeable in his playing, particularly under the recurring main guitar melody – lovingly dovetailed in the final rounds. The track fades to an end with the title being repeatedly called over a band jam.

'Whiskey in the Jar' (5:04) (Traditional)
Originally released by Thin Lizzy as a 1972 single
With a flourish of folky guitar and a chuggernaught rumble, this old Irish rock ballad springs into life and offers a fresh take on the Thin Lizzy standard. They don't quite make it their own as they did with Cave's 'Loverman' – this is a fairly traditional take – respect duly given to the reverence of the original, but there are glimpses of new character here, particularly Lars' great accenting on the kick and hi-hat during the 'musha-ring dum-a-doo dum-a-da' chorus sections. There's that gay abandon feel again. Four guys having the times of their lives, bashing out the songs they love and grew up with. Letting the song sing, not messing with or trying to rewrite the formula. It's all there for them, all they have to do is play it.

The second single plucked from the album and although failing to chart again back home, it hit a more than respectable number 29 in the UK. Whiskeys all round, then?

'Tuesday's Gone' (9:03) (Collins/Van Zahdt)
Originally released by Lynyrd Skynyrd on the *Pronounced Leh-nerd Skin-nerd* album, 1973
Recorded live as part of the KSJO FM 'Don't Call Us, We'll Call You' special on December 18, 1997, featuring Lynyrd Skynyrd guitarist Gary Rossington, John Popper from Blues Traveler, Les Claypool from Primus, Pepper Keenan from Corrosion of Conformity, ex-Faith No More guitarist Jim Martin and Alice in Chains' Jerry Cantrell and Sean Kinney
Metallica and the above friends joined together in late December 1997 as part of the *Reload* promotional vehicle, utilising the American airwaves to great effect. This Skynyrd track was, therefore, a natural inclusion for the follow-up album proper, both Hetfield and Newsted previously stating their deep-rooted love for the country folk rockers.

This performance has a jovial feel like old schoolmates banded together once more, reminiscing over old times. Although acoustically, this seems at odds with its bedfellows on this set, it works as a meandering, mood-changing detour from the heavy standards surrounding it.

'The More I See' (3:23) (Morris/Wainwright/Molaney/Roberts)
Originally released by Discharge as a 1984 single
Another homage to the thunderous UK rockers neatly closes the first disc. Slightly wordier than track one, it completes a satisfying circle of those early inspirations. Riffs to the wall and hell for leather – from small English town

roots to European satanic prophecies and everything in between – there's 'more to see' and hear on this album than you think.

Disc Two
Garage Days Re-Revisited '87
'Helpless' (6:36), 'The Small Hours' (6:39), 'The Wait' (4:55), 'Crash Course in Brain Surgery' (3:10), 'Last Caress/Green Hell' (3:28)

Garage Days Revisited '84
'Am I Evil?' (7:50)
This is the 'studio' cover version, version. Dubbed as part of a 'Garage Days Revisited' release on the flip side of the 'Creeping Death' 12" single to help promote the back end of the 'Ride the Lightning' tour in late 1984. As covers go, this is as faithful as they come; almost note for note true to the hallowed original.

'Blitzkrieg' (3:36) (Jones/Smith/Sirotto)
Originally released by Blitzkrieg as a B-side to the 1981 single 'Buried Alive'
Paired with 'Am I Evil?' as the other half of the 'Garage Days Revisited' release, there's a real 'Ain't My Bitch', *Load* feel to the verses. There's also a real live feel to proceedings here – bashed out in the studio in double-quick time – emphasised by a post-performance belch and Lars' admission that he might have slightly f*cked up a bit. Thankfully, they don't do the weird, laser effect sound ending of the original.

B-sides & One-Offs '88-'91
'Breadfan' (5:41) (Phillips/Shelley/Bourge)
Originally released by Budgie on the *Never Turn Your Back on a Friend* album, 1973
Recorded as part of the *Justice* sessions to help the band ease into a full album project and later released as a B-side to the 'Harvester of Sorrow' single. The driving riff roars this track into life, sounding like a motorbike revving into action. The original is a tad more pronounced and goes on slightly longer – almost a minute in total, to be exact. The breakdown features simply clean guitar instead of Budgie's acoustics. Chimes of 'Master of Puppets' can clearly be heard – birds of inspiration for sure.

'The Prince' (4:24) (Tatler/Harris)
Originally released by Diamond Head on the *Lightning to the Nations* album, 1980
Glam does speed metal. There's some ferocious soloing over breakneck drums in the intro and the pace never really lets up from start to finish. The 'other' track recorded as part of those initial *Justice* sessions, also featuring as a B-side to 'Harvester of Sorrow'. Budgie and Diamond Head – naturally.

'Stone Cold Crazy' (2:17) (Mercury/May/Taylor/Deacon)
Another 'studio' cover version, version. This one was released as that aforementioned B-side to 'Enter Sandman' as well as appearing on the 1990 *Elektra's 40ᵗʰ Anniversary* compilation.

This rendition retains all the raw crunch of the Queen original, as well as some thunderous Lars double kick pedals in the second verse and those extra Hetfield expletives we heard on *Live Shit*.

'So What' (3:08) (Exalt/Kulmer)
The third and final previously mentioned 'studio' cover version on this set, also included on the 'Unforgiven' vinyl and 'Sad but True' CD single releases. This sickening take holds just as much venom as the original – of which 10,000 copies were seized by UK authorities and destroyed under the Obscene Publications Act back in 1982 – from the Sex Pistol wannabes.

'Killing Time' (3:03) (Sweet Savage)
Originally released by Sweet Savage as a B-side to the 1981 single 'Take No Prisoners'
No doubt where the melody idea for the chorus of 'Struggle Within' came from listening to this – it can practically be sung out over the top of this one. Recorded around the same time as the studio version of 'So What', spawned from the marathon *Black Album* sessions and also released on the 'Unforgiven' vinyl and 'Sad but True' CD single releases.

Motorheadache '95
'Overkill' (4:05) (Kilmister/Clarke/Taylor)
Originally released by Motorhead on the *Overkill* album, 1979
During the *Load* recording sessions, when the band got the call about appearing at Motorhead Lemmy Kilmister's 50ᵗʰ birthday celebrations, tape was left rolling as they rehearsed up a suite of songs they hoped would do the big man proud. This has all the power and rage of the original, which of course, sounds like a carbon copy of 'Ace of Spades' – but we can't blame Metallica for that! Lars relishes the incessant pounding of the kit, especially in the closing segment. Also released as a B-side to the 'Hero of the Day' single.

'Damage Case' (3:40) (Kilmister/Clarke/Taylor/Farren)
Originally released by Motorhead on the *Overkill* album, 1979
A stomping groove runs through the centre of this track, Hetfield sounding like he's having a ball as he belts out the vocal – a pantomime villain goading the crowd for boos and hisses. It lacks the gruff tone of Lemmy, but they are hard shoes to fill after all. Released as another B-side to 'Hero of the Day'.

'Stone Dead Forever' (4:51) (Kilmister/Clarke/Taylor)
Originally released by Motorhead on the *Bomber* album, 1979
At times, this sounds like a 'proper' album cut rather than a straight-to-tape, live-from-the-studio floor take. Newsted brings the live feel home by barking home the track's title in the choruses, however. The third Motorhead cover to find a home as a 'Hero of the Day' B-side.

'Too Late Too Late' (3:12) (Kilmister/Clarke/Taylor)
Originally released by Motorhead as a B-side to the 1979 single 'Overkill'
It's never 'too late' for a Motorhead number and Hetfield conjures his innermost Lemmy for the final track on this rogue's gallery collection of covers – sounding more like him than ever before. A final tribute and the final Motorhead 'Hero of the Day' B-side release.

S&M (1999)

Personnel:
Kirk Hammett: guitars
James Hetfield: guitars, vocals
Jason Newsted: bass
Lars Ulrich: drums
Michael Kamen: conductor of the San Francisco Symphony Orchestra
Jeremy Constant (concertmaster), Melissa Kleinbart, Naomi Kazama, Victor Romasevich, Diane Nicholeris, Florin Parvulescu, Yukiko Kurakata, Kelly Leon-Pearce, Rudolph Kremer, Connie Gantsweg, Catherine Down and Philip Santos: first violinists
Paul Brancato (principal), Chumming Mo Kobialka, Kum Mo Kim, Enrique Bocedi, Michael Gerling, Yasuko Hattori, Frances Jeffrey, Bruce Freifeld, Daniel Kobiallka and Daniel Banner: second violinists
Geraldine Walther (principal), Yun Jie Liu, Don Ehrlich, Gina Feinauer, David Gaudry, Christina King, Seth Mausner and Nanci Severance: violas
David Teie (principal), Barara Bogatin, Jill Rachuy Brindel, David Goldblatt, Anne Pinsker, Peter Shelton, Judiyaba and Richard Andaya: violincellos
Larry Epstein (principal), Stephen Tramontozzi, William Ritchen, Chris Gilbert, S. Mark Wright and Charles Chandler: basses
Paul Renzi (principal), Linda Lukas and Catherine Payne: flutes
Eugene Izotov (principal), Pamela Smith and Julie Ann Giacobassi: oboes
Luis Beez (principal), Sheryl Renk and Anthony Striplen: clarinets
Stephen Paulson (principal), Rob Weir and Steven Braunstein: bassoons
Robert Ward (principal), Bruce Roberts, Jonathan Ring, Douglas Hull, Jim Smesler, Eric Achen and Joshua Garrett: horns
Glenn Fischthal (principal), Craig Morris, Chris Bogios and Andrew McCandless: trumpets
Paul Welcomer (principal), Tom Hornig, Jeffrey Budin and John Engelkes: trombones
Peter Wahrhaftig: tuba
Douglas Rioth: harp
David Herbert: timpani
Raymond Froehlich (principal), Anthony J. Cirone, Tom Hemphill and Artie Storch: percussion
Marc Shapiro: keyboard
Recorded live at: Berkeley Community Theatre, Berkeley, California on 21 and 22 April 1999, using Effanel Music and Westwood One mobile recording trucks
Producer: Bob Rock with Hetfield and Ulrich and Michael Kamen
Release date: 23 November 1999
Chart placings: US: 2, UK: 33
Label: Elektra (US), Vertigo (UK)

After cancelling part of the 'Poor ReTouring Me' tour in September 1998 to work on the *Garage Inc.* album, Metallica hit the stage again on 18 October at none other than the Playboy Mansion in LA, appearing at a private party hosted by South Park creators Trey Parker and Matt Stone for the release of the duo's Orgazmo movie. The 'Garage Barrage' tour then cranked into life on 17 November in Toronto, Canada, morphing into a run of 'Garage Remains the Same' shows in 1999, which kicked off in Mexico City (one of the previously cancelled shows) the week after two nights of these ground-breaking *S&M* performances with the San Francisco Symphony Orchestra.

'Conducting a conversation between two different worlds that share the language of music', is how conductor Michael Kamen described this project in September 1999 – succinctly put. Symphony and Metallica may not have worked after all – but it *really* does.

Hetfield put it rather differently when speaking about the juxtaposition of the collaboration at the time – 'we have a passion in our music and our music is our life. They just grew up learning it different'.

On closer listen, many of Metallica's compositions have symphonic, cinematic qualities about them. The epic and grandiose 'Ktulu', the sweeping 'Fade to Black' and of course, the all-encompassing, fan-attracting 'Nothing Else Matters'. A classically trained musician at heart, original bassist Cliff Burton is often cited by his fellow band members as bringing lots of these attributes to the group. Heavy, dark and menacing much of their music may be, but underneath, if you drill down, they are songs at heart and songs that are wonderfully augmented by the strings, bows, horns and wider ensemble of the San Francisco Symphony here.

Using an orchestra to embellish and transform rock music has been done before, of course – think Deep Purple's *Concerto For Group And Orchestra* or Rick Wakeman's grandiose *Journey To The Centre Of The Earth* – but never perhaps using material quite this alternative and/or aggressive. It was a gamble for sure, but one that Kamen thought would pay off after first being introduced to Metallica by Bob Rock during the *Black Album* sessions, when he was asked to score an arrangement for 'Nothing Else Matters'.

Years later, the band jumped at the chance to try something a bit different when Kamen approached them with an idea for a full-on project and the *S&M* fetish was born.

Fronted by Michael Kamen, who sadly passed away in November 2003 after suffering a heart attack, he brought all the credentials. Conductor at Roger Waters' ambitious *Wall – Live in Berlin*, musical director for the Queen's Golden Jubilee celebrations at Buckingham Palace and a prolific film and TV music composer – he certainly fitted the bill. Immersing himself in all things Metallica for six months prior to three rehearsals (two with the band), Kamen scored the arrangements for all 21 tracks included here, which for all intents and purposes, is almost a greatest hits collection with a couple of new additions thrown in to keep the hungry-for-new-material fans satisfied. A two-CD set was simultaneously released with a DVD – in glorious 5.1 surround sound – and VHS, featuring a 41-minute behind-the-scenes documentary on the making of the project.

The album artwork features Hetfield, stage front with head chopped off, Kamen to his right and Newsted to his left in front of the orchestra. A new, neat, white *S&M* logo sits on top of a stave that runs underneath. The inlay features an essay from Kamen about the project, along with numerous colour photos of the shows from Anton Corbijn again.

Disc One
'The Ecstasy of Gold' (2:30)
Always a brilliant start to any Metallica show but played live and exclusively by the San Francisco Symphony makes it sound even more immense. The introductory trumpet and ringing bell lend an authentic sound to this Metalli-mood setter.

'The Call of the Ktulu' (9:34)
The roar of the crowd is audible as some of the band members appear on stage to open with this 'monster' track from *Ride* – I mean, what else? The three-note orchestral refrain over the main riff makes it sound more menacing than ever, but it's Lars' playing that really hits home – particularly in the building end sections – he's up for this.

'Master of Puppets' (8:54)
There's no let-up as we crash straight into a full-length version – not being short-changed here. The crowd play along with the call-and-response verses brilliantly, hollering out the lines in unison. It sounds like the soundtrack to the most horrific horror film you've ever seen, especially Hetfield's pleas of 'master' just before the instrumental section – orchestra crying along with him – as if begging for mercy. He laughs manically at the end to bring it to a close – someone else also having a good time.

'Of Wolf and Man' (4:18)
The horror continues with this genius inclusion – Newsted augments the vocals with some great background growling and the midsection howling wolves part sounds particularly disturbing in these surroundings.

'The Thing That Should Not Be' (7:26)
A cunning ploy is utilised here as the intro sounds like it's going to be 'Roam' from the *Black Album* – then it hits you – wallop! Working brilliantly with the orchestrations again, this *Puppetz* classic continues a real animalistic feel to proceedings. Hetfield plays the lead role excellently here – acting out vocals with real aplomb like it's a Broadway show. One of his finest live recorded vocals for me. The ending lingers, then smashes straight into …

'Fuel' (4:35)

The orchestra pounds out the riffs in tandem and it's a wall of relentless gasoline-charged sound – the crowd loving every second. This track is a fine example of how the orchestra complements the existing music so well. Working alongside, not against.

'The Memory Remains' (4:42)

Another more recent addition follows and it's great to hear the crowd singing along again. They take up Marianne Faithfull's vocal melody with consummate ease, long into the outro with the strings fading until ...

'No Leaf Clover' (5:43)

Fresh meat here, with great use of effects on Hetfield's vocals over the understated chorus sections. The wailing lead guitar at the end with Lars' drumming is a highlight – pounding relentlessly into the end stages.

The second and final single released from this album. Failing to chart in the UK – hitting a forgettable 74 in the US.

'Hero of the Day' (4:44)

Another track which works well with the full orchestra – really bringing out its melodic nature – particularly in the opening sections. It fairly packs its knockout punch when in full flow towards the end, though. Newsted on excellent backing vocal duty again too.

'Devil's Dance' (5:26)

Newsted takes up the mantle again here, working brilliantly with the orchestra in the intro. A faithful rendition, sounding much like the original *Reload* version, brings 'part one' to a conclusion by introducing a really ...

'Bleeding Me' (9:01)

... smooth and evolving version. Smooth because the guitars are played so lovingly, evolving because as things progress it builds and builds to a satisfying climax – more so than the original for me.

Disc Two
'Nothing Else Matters' (6:47)

After a brief interlude (for a sausage roll and a grin), we regroup for the lead single from this album – of course it was – released a day before the album. Another clever marketing ploy.

Their most accessible song, backed by a professional orchestra, what's not to love? Nothing, as it quite poetically turns out – yet it failed to chart on either side of the Atlantic – guess you can't win 'em all.

'Until it Sleeps' (4:29)

Arguably their other more recent, most 'accessible' tune. Newsted really gives it some on the backing vocals again here – he's getting pretty good at this.

'For Whom the Bell Tolls' (4:52)

This is a rampant, and I mean truly rampant, rendition. As if they're saying: 'hey, don't you forget who we are! We're f*cking Metallica!', the orchestra embellish this song more than any other. The 'it's the last time you will!' section really makes the hairs stand up on the back of your neck. A tumultuous end brings us another new track and another highlight from this performance.

'-Human' (4:19)

Using all the drama from the orchestra right from the intro, bleeding perfectly into Metallica's style, the verses are particularly hooky and strong, as is Lars' tom and hi-hat work throughout them. The lazy-like cymbal work continues in the chorus and there's a genius, drawn-out 'breathe' at the very end to tease it out.

'Wherever I May Roam' (7:01)

The orchestra draw out all the cinematic grandeur during the intro, building up to a riotous rendition of this *Black Album* stalwart. The crowd come into their own towards the end, shouting out the 'wanders' with true passion and devotion.

'Outlaw Torn' (9:58)

A stomping attack. Hetfield's vocals really shine here – sounding strong and clear – cutting through all the mayhem brilliantly.

'Sad but True' (5:46)

Another *Black Album* favourite sets up a magnificent sequence to end. Newsted whips up the crowd during the intro and continues during the instrumental/breakdown section.

'One' (7:53)

When the gunfire heralds the start, the string section soon adds more cinematic flavour – sweeping the intro and verses into the hellish nightmare of its final stages.

'Enter Sandman' (7:39)

This brings the party – everyone's been waiting for it and in these surroundings, it sounds even more groundbreaking than before. The orchestra takes centre stage for a while before the final rousing end riff sections.

'Battery' (7:24)

To end with this is just piling on the pressure. It's a furious version and I imagine the orchestra members were run ragged by it. Never in the history of classical music has a violinist ever been so keen to put down their bow – and need to blow out the flames before they do. Emphatic.

Part Four: The Anger: 2003 to 2023
St. Anger (2003)
Personnel:
Kirk Hammett: guitars
James Hetfield: guitars, vocals
Bob Rock: bass
Lars Ulrich: drums
Recorded at: HQ, San Rafael, California, between May 2002 and April 2003
Producer: Bob Rock and Metallica
Release date: 5 June 2003
Chart placings: US: 1, UK: 3
Label: Elektra (US), Vertigo (UK)
All songs on this album are written by Hetfield/Ulrich/Hammett/Rock

'The Garage Remains the Same' shows ran into July 1999, finishing with a headline spot at Woodstock in Griffis Park, New York, on the 24th. After a brief break, touring reconvened, imaginatively titled 'M2K'; with the band careering into a new century, with new sounds and collaborations behind them, fans were left wondering what a new dawn had in store for them. Where to go next? What kind of Metallica?

First up was a dabble in the movies with the release of the 'I Disappear' single on 26 June 2000, which featured in the *Mission Impossible 2* blockbusting film. They took up the touring mantle again a few days later – prior to premiering their new track at the MTV Movie Awards on 3 June – a spate of 'Summer Sanitarium' shows seeing out the year in suitable style.

The end of 2000 heralded more change than could be imagined, however, and another award show appearance, namely the VH1 My Music bash on 30 November, turned out to be Newsted's last appearance with the band. On 17 January 2001, an official statement read 'that after fourteen years as Metallica's bass player, Jason has chosen to leave'. Cited for 'private and personal reasons' and down to 'physical damage' he'd done to himself, it was another critical blow to the rhythm section. The more deep-rooted, creative frustration reasonings would soon become more apparent and documented. Newsted carried on with his side project Echobrain – a departure that had previously not gone down too well with fellow Metallica members, Hetfield in particular, who had likened the bassist's dabbles to cheating on his wife.

Seemingly undaunted, the band set to work on the new album on 23 April, but sessions were halted on 19 July while Hetfield checked into rehabilitation to exorcise his own Metalli-demons. They reconvened in May 2002 with renewed vigour and a new Hetfield to set about the arduous task of completing the album.

With only two shows in the diary for 2002 and with producer Bob Rock filling in on bass duties for the meantime, auditions were duly held, culminating in Robert Trujillo (10.23.64) officially joining the band on 24 February 2003. A friend of many years, the ex-Suicidal Tendencies and Ozzy Osbourne bassist had previously done the rounds supporting Metallica on their early 1990s tours – a good fit and a natural choice then. Not so natural was one of his first appearances – San Quentin State Prison on 1 May – to film the video for the title track single and album release promotion, quite the baptism indeed.

Back to the album, and after the classical nature of *S&M*, *St. Anger* is certainly a shock to the system. No polished hard rock feel here, the production is toned down and what you hear is what it is: a constant, unrelenting barrage of guitars and drums. Noise, pure and simple. It hits you from the first second and doesn't let up throughout its 75 minutes and six seconds runtime. Metallica come from thrash to (p)rock to harder rock and now to some kind of alt/industrial style metal – with one wicked and harsh-sounding snare drum. The drums sound like no other on this album – metal on metal – and the guitars attack with anger. As Hetfield put it:

St. Anger was pretty much a statement – it felt like the purging of a feeling… us working together – in harmony, in friction, in happiness, in sadness… all of that put together. And we're able to get through it – we've walked through the fire; we know how hot it can get, and we don't need to go there again.

Remember wondering how Newsted felt on *Justice* when he couldn't hear his bass? Well on this, there isn't a single guitar solo if I'm not mistaken. It's not everyone's cup of tea, but it's so far removed from the *Load*-era sound that it makes it even more fascinating.

The title track is hands down one of my all-time favourite Metallica tunes – probably number four. It's just so 'angry' and relentless and from 45 seconds when all hell is breaking loose, it quite simply does not get any better.

The critics were universally complimentary on the whole, *Rolling Stone* hailing it as 'something they had to do in order to hold themselves together' and describing it as 'raw sounds… as if the band members (are) focused solely on playing off one and other, not the mixing board… too busy to notice that the snare drum annoyingly goes ping instead of snap'. Elsewhere, the UK's *NME (New Musical Express)* suggested that 'anger isn't just used as an outlet and energy… but romanticised as a full-bloodied emotion' and that 'musically, the songs are a stripped back, heroically brutal reflection of (this) fury'. Just a shame the reviewer back then spelt Newstead's name wrong – disrespectful.

The album artwork, designed by the band themselves, is another departure. Matt Mahurin's striking red fist adorns the front cover, tied by rope at the wrist. The back cover features graphic artist Pushead's hellish-looking skull, complete with straggled black hair and yellowing teeth – the fist from the front tellingly tied around its neck. Inside we get more Anton Corbijn band photography and more illustrations, namely a tortured and bound demon, which depicts the 'Unnamed Feeling' album track. In addition to the main release, the CD also featured a DVD of full live rehearsal performances of each track. This is not music for the fainthearted and is a gruelling listen all in one go.

'Frantic' (5:50)

The assault on the senses is instant, as pummelling stabs of guitar and drums bring the album crashing into life. But it's the drum sound that floors you at first: industrial sounding, tinny and abrasive. The main 'live it or lie it' guitar and bass refrain then brings everyone driving towards the first verse: 'If I could have my wasted days back, would I use them to get back on track?' sings Hetfield. Our frontman exorcising more of his demons on record. The 'frantic, tick, tick, tick, tick, tick, tock' is a clever play on words in the choruses – then from 3:46, the guitars come furiously together to usher in a final bridge/chorus run before four stabs of guitar and drums send us careering to the end.

Released as the album's second single on 15 September 2003 – it failed to chart in the States but reached number 16 in the UK.

'St. Anger' (7:21)

If the anger wasn't clear enough from the previous track, here it is in all its rage and glory.

An evil guitar riff introduces a very bassy-sounding Lars floor tom before more clanging stabs announce a marching stomp. But from 44 seconds in, the pace dramatically quickens and listeners are engulfed in a maelstrom of frantic(tock) guitars and lightning speed double kick pedals from Lars. It's a relief when the hooky verse section comes in – Hetfield's voice sounds clear and true. The chorus is hooky, too – again at breakneck speed and with expletives for good measure.

The formula is repeated, but from 5:20, we get the real crux of this track: 'I need my anger not to control' growls Hetfield – 'SET ME FREE!' – which cues a complete and utter metal mayhem to end.

The lead single – of course. Released on 23 June 2003, and although failing to chart back home, reached a remarkable UK high of 9. Back with an angry BANG! Just brilliant.

'Some Kind of Monster' (8:25)

There's a real studio floor, live feel to the intro here – rather akin to the *$5.98 E.P.* previously. Some pounding drums then introduce a surprising lead guitar riff (few and far between on this album), but it's not until 2:07 that we get a vocal.

There's more impressive Lars tom runs over the second 'silence no more' section, then more high-speed drumming before the 'monster' chorus comes lumbering along. The riff is heavy and animalistic – 'this monster lives'.

Clever wordplay from 6:57, with an evil 'ominous/I'm-in-us' chant, takes us into the final chorus. We finish with another studio floor, improvised-sounding flurry.

The fourth and final single (US only) from the album – failed to chart.

'Dirty Window' (5:24)
Straight off the back of a monster comes some frenetic guitar and drum stabs and we're soon away on a hooky riff and into the first verse. It's the chorus that's king here though when some Lars rimshots announce Hetfield in all his metal prowess – 'projector, rejector, infector, defector'. He's loving it, especially at 3:59 when he cackles over the deafening stabs, taking us into the final 'cup of denial' stages.

'Invisible Kid' (8:30)
A commercial-sounding verse melody sits awkwardly over a bedrock of more furious metal from 54 seconds in, after a quite monstrously impenetrable intro. In another world – probably Bob Rock's – this might well have been the lead single, as after the soulful 'I'm OK, just go away' section, the commerciality returns with the 'open your heart, I'm beating right here' chorus. Of course, what isn't chart-friendly and commercial is the next segment (or the track's length), as things slow down and we enter more familiar 'angrier' territory. In fact, from 5:04 and the pained Hetfield vocal – 'ooh, unplugging from it all (wish they would), invisible kid floats alone in his room' – you practically beg for the end. The lyrics aren't particularly chart-friendly either, telling a tale of some insular character locked away and left ostracised by society: 'Never see what he did, got stuck where he hid, fallen through the grid. Got a place of his own, where he'll never be known, inward he's grown'.

If ever there was a single remix required, this one ticks the box.

'My World' (5:45)
There's more accessibility here, particularly in the chorus sections – Lars' tom runs surrounding some catchy vocals. There's even a poppy 'sucker' thrown in after the final hi-hat bash. This is one track that sits slightly at odds with the rest of the album – not throwaway, but certainly not as sprawling and toxic as the music it surrounds. They bring back the anger a little from 3:18, however, all piling in together with Hetfield shouting the odds – 'not only do I not know the answer, I don't even know what the question is'. Kind of summing this album up on all fronts so far. 'Enough's enough'.

'Shoot Me Again' (7:10)
Some scratchy fretwork brings in a very 'Some Kind of Monster' riff. A track that sounds like its bastard child in places. There's some brilliant space in the chorus, particularly after Hetfield goads us to pull the trigger – the staccato

'all the shots' hitting hard and right where it hurts. From 5:14, a prehistoric riff takes hold and drives towards the end with a final 'all the shots' – this time without the space – and Lars has had enough; the drums must die!

'Sweet Amber' (5:27)

A very lazy, almost clean-sounding guitar introduces a driving riff to announce a tale of toking and smoking. The fumes unfurl around us at the 'ooh then she holds my hand' section, before knocking us out. Lars' cymbals wash over the mix to conjure the perfect picture. A recurring 'St. Anger' riff also permeates this track at times – themes and motifs returning to underline the overall concept. Nice work.

'The Unnamed Feeling' (7:08)

Like the 'Monster' before it, there's yet another dark and disturbing feel to this, raising its ugly head from one minute in – a 'been here before' vocal screeching out over the guitar and drums. At 2:17, the noise subsides a little and a clean guitar allows Lars to groove us back into the carnage, which erupts as Hetfield pleads with us to 'go away' in very certain terms at 4:56, bringing us into a full band chorus to end.

This feels like (along with the title track) the crux of the album and there's a real cinematic soundtrack theme – although, funnily enough, 'Some Kind of Monster' would ultimately turn out to become a track title used in a film.

Nevertheless, this one was released as part of an EP on 12 January 2004 – the third pick from the album. It failed to chart again back home but reached number 42 in the UK. It would most probably have fared better paired as a double A-side with 'St. Anger'.

'Purify' (5:13)

The disjointed, jumbled nature of this track seems to perfectly encapsulate the overall theme and concept of this album. Never knowing quite what to expect or where it will turn, apart from the constant noise and aggression. The driving chorus probably ties it up better than most, however, until at 4:38, when an almost *Kill 'Em All*-esque riff drives us headlong to the final track.

'All Within My Hands' (8:48)

Lars isn't finished with us yet. His pounding snare drum brings out the worst in his bandmates as they rock out an extended intro into a groovy verse. The guitar picking of the bridge section then halts suddenly to announce the pre-chorus – into a barrage of 'hate me now' repetitions before a lazy, shifting, rumbling riff. There's a moment's respite at 5:04 before another riff of ages comes growling out of the feedback to set Lars off on another rampage.

The end is suitably emphatic; 'kill, kill, kill' ringing out over the now, horribly familiar unrelenting guitars and drums. Then it's all over – time to get your ears back. What a ride!

Interestingly, the track's title was later used as the name for a foundation set up by the band in 2017, 'dedicated to creating sustainable communities by supporting workforce education, the fight against hunger, and other critical local services'. Portions of show ticket sales were donated to chosen local initiatives at every tour stop across the world, including homeless charities, food banks and humanitarian organisations, to name just a few. Ironic, really when you consider some of the lyrics on offer from the track itself: 'squeeze it in, crush it down, hold it dear... suffocate/love to death, smack you 'round & 'round, beware'. But maybe that's the point.

Death Magnetic (2008)

Personnel:
Kirk Hammett: guitars
James Hetfield: guitars, vocals
Robert Trujillo: bass
Lars Ulrich: drums
Recorded at: Sound City Studios, Van Nuys, California, Shangri La Studios, Malibu, California and HQ, San Rafael, California, between April 2007 and May 2008
Producer: Rick Rubin
Release date: 12 September 2008
Chart placings: US: 1, UK: 1
Label: Warner Bros. (US), Vertigo (UK)
All songs on this album are written by Hetfield/Ulrich/Hammett/Trujillo

The 'Summer Sanitarium 2003' tour kicked off on 4 July at the Pontiac Silverdome in Michigan, running until 10 August at Candlestick Park in San Francisco.

A number of planned dates were then cancelled in October/November due to 'physical and mental exhaustion', but Metallica were back on stage, somewhat surprisingly, in Tokyo, Japan, on 6 November and saw out the year at The Joint in Las Vegas on New Year's Eve, a show which featured no less than three encores – no wonder they were so tired!

2004 began with a stint in New Zealand and Australia before the 'Madly in Anger With the World' tour kicked off in earnest on 27 February at the Cow Palace in San Francisco.

Exhaustion didn't seem to be a recurring problem as the tour had no less than 108 dates, culminating in an appearance at the HP Pavilion, San Jose, California. Running at around two-and-a-half hours, each show was presented in 'the round' with audiences experiencing full Metalli-mania up close and personal. With incessant touring finally catching up with them again, 2005 was deemed a 'year off', save two shows supporting none other than The Rolling Stones at SBC Park in San Fransisco on 13 and 15 November.

The turbulent times of the last few years had finally been laid bare with the release of the warts and all documentary *Some Kind of Monster* – a hard-hitting, no holds barred examination of life inside the juggernaut that is Metallica. Released in January 2005, it's a fascinating snapshot of the real struggles and realities of the writing and recording process for *St. Anger*. From the true creative frustrations that drove Newsted to pastures new, through to Hetfield confronting his inner vices and demons and decisions on whether or not the band would even continue – it's all there. An absolute must-watch for any long-time fan, which also portrays the difficulties Kirk has faced over the years – struggling to appease and often reconcile the constant locking of horns between Hetfield and Ulrich – it's a wonder he stuck around for so long. Bless him. A two-DVD set contained seven hours of bonus features, exclusive interviews, audio commentaries, trailers and a music video.

Most of the next year was spent writing and rehearsing material for a new album, with only a handful of live shows on the calendar – 17 in total. A 'new song' was teasingly debuted at the Waldbuhne, Berlin, Germany on 6 June, then it was back in the studio between festival appearances and one-off shows in 2007 – notably a headline night at London's Wembley Stadium (their first) and a return to Moscow, Russia (16 years on) at the Luzhniki Stadium – dubbed the 'Sick of the Studio '07' tour.

After the harsh aggressiveness of *St. Anger*, it almost feels like a back-to-basics approach was adopted for the new material and with a new producer, Rick Rubin (Slayer/System of a Down), in charge too. Many of the early Metallica hallmarks rear their heads again across a series of tightly woven, progressive, and at times, grandiose, hard rock cuts. Shades of *Lightning*, *Puppetz* and even *Black* pepper the album. According to Lars:

With *St. Anger* nobody brought in any pre-recorded stuff or ideas, it was just make it up on the spot, be in the moment. So this time, we are doing exactly what we did on all the other albums: first, we're writing, then we're recording. The only difference is that we're writing where we record... at HQ because this is our home.

So, are they still pissed off? Maybe not quite so much this time, but aggressiveness still prevails on this album; there's no doubt about it.

With a heartbeat intro into an eerie guitar, it is a clear sign from the start of 'That Was Just Your Life' (track one) that this is no *St. Anger*.

There's a hint of that classic Metallica in 'Day That Never Comes' (track four) – almost 'Fade to Black' like in its majesty and with a furious outro that could just go on and on.

'All Nightmare Long' (track five) continues the quality, with a 'Sandman' style start and there's even an instrumental thrown in for good measure. We haven't had one for ages, and when they're as strong as 'Suicide & Redemption' (track nine), you have to ask yourself why?

The artwork is black on white – a buried, open coffin surrounded by black soil swirls sits below a silver (classic) Metallica logo and album title. The inlay features the now obligatory Anton Corbijn band photography, with the coffin cleverly punching a hole through each page – lyrics and all.

The album's title is partly in recognition of fellow musicians who have paid the ultimate price for following the rock and roll dream, as Hetfield explained:

Thinking about death... some people are drawn towards it... just like a magnet, and other people are afraid of it. Also, the concept that we're all gonna die sometimes is over-talked about and then a lot of times never talked about – no one wants to bring it up; it's the big white elephant in the room. But we all have to deal with it at some point.

'That Was Just Your Life' (7:10)

Out of the screaming anger comes a gentle, beating heart. Differences put aside, perhaps? After all the drama and turmoil of the previous few years, is this another new Metallica emerging from a cocoon of bitterness and hate?

A clean but disturbing picked refrain soon bursts into drums and guitar stabs, before we're off on a *Kill 'Em All*-esque riff from 1:27. The pace soon quickens, as does Lars' bass drum pedals before Hetfield launches into an almost metal rap. He spits out the words in double-quick time, at times sounding like he's struggling to keep pace with the grinding rhythm guitar: 'Like a face that learns to speak when all it knew was how to bite'.

At 2:18, they break into a 'Blackened' sounding section, then a half-speed chugging riff sounds brilliantly at odds with the vocal phrasing – shifting and lazy. The chorus vocal melody is catchy and commercial and bleeds brilliantly back into the verse sections again – Lars announcing them with some on-point, military-style snare fills. Kirk's solo comes screaming out of the speakers at 4:52, again sounding very much like early Metallica. This is back to basics but not the basic raw sound of *St. Anger*. This sound is full and full of life as Lars pummels the kick and cymbals heading into the final chorus.

'The End of the Line' (7:50)

After a stop-start intro, a chugging riff and some lingering cymbals announce a *Load*-style guitar pattern before morphing into a 'Seek & Destroy' sounding breakdown. This sounds like an amalgamation of early and latter Metallica, all stirred up in a melting pot of modern-day metal. The staccato, slightly out-of-time rhythm of the chorus, 'you've – reached – the – end – of – the – line', is a clever way to complete the song cycle. Some dualling guitar riffs then lead into a suitably 'wah-wah-ing' Kirk solo before it breaks down slightly again, drawing us into a clean-sounding and disturbing end section. 'The slave becomes the master' lyric builds and builds until Hetfield explodes into the final stages – Lars' double kick adding extra power.

'Broken, Beat & Scarred' (6:25)

Some great tom work from Lars ushers in the full band and a classic-sounding riff, the snare drum fills, taking control of the structure at the start. The commercial-sounding nature of the verses cannot be denied – 'what don't kill ya, make you more strong'. The drums really take charge here, from pounding snare and toms, through to the double kick playing of the 'show your scars' passage. The pace quickens at 3:50, setting up a manic Kirk solo over some driving riffs. The drums then take over again, hurling us into the final chorus section.

The third and final single from the album failed to chart both at home and in the UK.

'The Day That Never Comes' (7:55)

'Fade to Black' oozes all through the intro here – we're riding the lightning again. A lovely clean guitar section sits underneath some heartfelt Hetfield vocals. His tone is great – crooning yet believable. The haunting main riff recurs after another Lars-driven chorus flourish – a clean guitar-picking pattern that threads through the entire opening section.

The old, multiple-song-in-one-card trick is then forcibly brandished from 3:58 as the 'love is a four-letter word' section is driven home. Then the pace dramatically picks up as Hetfield blasts out 'this I swear!' – duelling guitars battling once again in-between some tight riffing. Kirk takes over to lead out the final stages before all hell breaks loose a 7:48 to bring proceedings to a dramatic and dead stop.

The lead single release from the album. It reached 31 in the US and a better 19 in the UK. My favourite track on this album – cos the old tricks are always the best!

'All Nightmare Long' (8:01)

A great drum and bass partnership kicks things off here – lumbering out of the sudden silence of the previous track's end. But from 37 seconds, everyone joins the party as the track comes rumbling into full life. Hetfield growls a studio floor 'one, two' at 1:14, but it's not until 1:46 that a sparse lead vocal kicks in – three words – 'luck runs out'. After some deathly chugging, the chorus is announced with a blast of the snare drum and the full force hits you. So catchy, so singable – and 'single'-ble too, as it so happens. Hetfield is relishing his vocal role here again and you can hear it with the way he hangs playfully on the 'ts' of the 'luck runs ouT' lyric in the chorus. In the second stage of the song, Kirk comes fully to life. Gone are the chains of the 'no solos allowed' ethos of the previous album and he rocks out with his bandmates to full aplomb, nowhere more so than at the 5:17 mark. Another joyful count – this time a 'one, two, three (and a) four' – from Hetfield eventually sets Lars off on more double kick duties, then after a pinpoint two-second dead stop, the final chorus comes satisfyingly screaming out of the silence.

The second single release from the album. Again, and this time somewhat surprisingly, it failed to chart on either side of the Atlantic.

'Cyanide' (6:41)

That wah-wah guitar effect is employed to great effect over stabs of drums and guitars, before the drums and bass lock together again over the intro here. A distorted effect on Trujillo's bass pairs wonderfully with Lars' driving rhythm. Another *Load*-flavoured riff then introduces the verse before yet another commercial-sounding bridge crosses over into the chorus. The outright stomp of the 'suicide, I've already died' section begs to be played out in a stadium. But there's more ... and with a flurry of *Justice*-style offbeat stabs over the snare, then toms, a cleaner groovier section comes in. Kirk fights over the relentless pounding from 4:08, building to an inevitable crescendo and final bridge and chorus.

'The Unforgiven III' (7:47)

The trilogy is complete – but wait – no hornpipe? Alas, it is replaced here by a soothing piano melody (with trumpet at least) until an even more haunting bassy riff starts the song proper. There are hints of the previous two instalments, particularly when the first verse kicks in – that wall of sound grinding against the vocal, although not quite as pronounced as part one. The lyrics of the chorus are just as heartbreaking – 'how can I be lost, if I've got nowhere to go?/how can I blame you, when it's me I can't forgive?'

There is real heartache here and from 4:41, over the most lonesome-sounding lead guitar, it all comes to a head: 'Forgive me – forgive me not' pleads Hetfield. He's in absolute turmoil and when Lars' toms start to build, he gets close to breaking point before the rhythm quickens and he finally does – screaming out, 'why can't I forgive me!' over an insurmountable wall of noise and lead guitar. When it's all done with, all that's left is a final sorrowful verse/chorus, the book finally closing (for now) on a tragedy of epic proportions.

Confusingly not released as a single anywhere – would've been nice ...

'The Judas Kiss' (8:02)

The drive, almost swing, of the final chorus stages is the crux of this track, but before all that comes a half-time, staggering verse and a hit-single-ridden bridge. All three are, at times, hard to separate over the course of the song but are bound together by an extended instrumental passage from 4:25. You can't but fail to hear Newsted goading the crowds with 'heys!' – but that is from another life. Then at 4:52, Kirk flicks the switch to 'hit the lights' with his lightning-fast fingers as the new Metallica drive headlong into a telling lyric: 'Judas lives, recite this vow – I've become your new god now!' Surely no one can deny this band's refreshing new direction – not even 'him'. He'd struggle as well because the soloing isn't finished just yet, not before Lars breaks things down on the toms and Hetfield growls from the depths into the final chorus. Last suppers all round, please!

'Suicide & Redemption' (10:02)

An instrumental which sounds similar to *Justice*'s 'To Live is to Die' – a chance for Trujillo to stretch his new bass muscles, perhaps? This he does to great effect during a fade-in intro, before the chugging leads in a monster riff and some harmonic guitars. At 3:39, the ghost of Cliff fully resonates in a clean-sounding *Puppetz* section, but it's not long before the grinding guitars and harmonics reappear. Then at 5:24, Trujillo retakes the crown to signal a build-up into a lead guitar break over the double-timed main riff. It all comes crashing down at 7:48, back into the main theme, before some improvised drums take us meandering out to fade.

'My Apocalypse' (5:01)

The back-to-basics 'garage days' ethos of this album is never more evident than in this final track. It's outright gay abandon, hell for leather playing from the start, with an album title namedrop in the second verse for good measure: 'Deadly vision, prophecy reveal. Death magnetic, pulling closer still'.

There's a real *Puppetz* 'Battery' feel throughout, a sense of bringing the collection to a close with little left in the tank until the next time – the next show. Like an encore they never want to end, they career into the final stuttering apocalypses until Lars heralds the end with deafening kick and cymbals – curtain down, game over.

Metallica Through the Never (2013)

Personnel:
Kirk Hammett: guitars
James Hetfield: guitars, vocals
Robert Trujillo: bass
Lars Ulrich: drums
Recorded at: Rexall Place, Edmonton, Alberta on 17 and 18 August 2012 and
Rogers Arena, Vancouver, British Columbia on 24, 25 and 27 August 2012.
Producer: Greg Fidelman
Release date: 24 September 2013
Chart placings: US: 9, UK: 36
Label: Blackened Recordings

The *World Magnetic* tour kicked off on 21 October 2008 at the Jobing Arena, in Glendale Arizona and ran into November 2010 – an impressive 182 shows in total.

En route, the band were inducted into the hallowed US 'Rock and Roll Hall of Fame' and celebrated in fine fashion with a 25th-anniversary performance at Madison Square Garden on 30 October 2009 alongside fellow Hall of Famers U2, Jeff Beck, Ozzy Osborne (Black Sabbath) and Lou Reed (more to come of Lou later).

After such a gargantuan world tour and with previous burnout issues still a worry, 2011 was pencilled in as a recuperation period. Nevertheless, they still managed 22 dates across the world, including some 'Big 4' (Metallica/Megadeth/Slayer/Anthrax) shows at Knebworth, UK (with Diamond Head in support), Canada, Brazil and even Delhi, India.

There was also the small matter of a collaborative project with the aforementioned Lou Reed, who'd been seduced by the band's energy and commitment at the Madison Square Garden gig. A fairly inaccessible and uncomfortable premise – the dark and troubled misadventures of a 19th Century French prostitute called Lulu – it offered a different creative outlet for the band members across a meandering, progressive, double-album set, featuring Reed's mumbling rants over a series of mostly improvised, cinematic flavoured jams. A relative commercial flop, it still didn't stop the marketing juggernaut and was promoted across four TV show-style appearances with Reed himself through Europe in the November of 2011. Creative juices firmly quenched, they saw out the year in style with four dates at The Fillmore in San Francisco celebrating their own 30th Anniversary. Friends on the nights included Alice in Chains' Jerry Cantrell, Glenn Danzig, Animal from Anti-Nowhere League and former brother Newsted, who joined them for performances of 'Harvester of Sorrow', 'Damage, Inc.', Seek & Destroy', 'Creeping Death' and 'Battery' among others. There was just time for four previously unreleased *Death Magnetic* session tracks to see the light of day, with *Beyond Magnetic* hitting laptops (iTunes), CD racks and turntables from 13 December.

After a break in the first quarter of 2012, the band arranged their own music festival – 'Orion Music + More' – two dates at Bader Field in Atlantic City, New Jersey, on 23 and 24 June. Headlining each night and playing *Ride the Lightning* and the *Black Album* in their entireties, it was a celebration of tastes and influences, including appearances from Sepultura, Suicidal Tendencies and UK indie band Arctic Monkeys, to name just a few.

An ambitious run of eight shows then followed at the Palacio de los Deportes in Mexico, some of which were used as rehearsals for what would later become the bones of this next live release – *Through the Never* – the soundtrack to the film of the same name. Directed by Nimrod Antal, the movie tells the avant-garde tale of a fictional Metallica roadie (Dane Deehan) on a quest to protect the band from a murderous apocalyptic horseman – all set to the backdrop of the live performances. All the band got on board with the project, with each member credited with screenplay writing.

2012 ended with the creation of their own record label – Blackened Recordings of course!

The new year then heralded festival dates in Australia, before moving on to Abu Dhabi, South Africa, Japan, China and South Korea ahead of the full release of the *Through the Never* movie in IMAX theatres at the end of September.

The audio release is notable for including full-length live versions of the first three album title tracks (not in order) – 'Ride the Lightning', '...And Justice For All' and 'Master of Puppets' – a nice collector's edition for fans and a souvenir of 2012's summer 'Full Arsenal' tour, which had featured the band's own 'all new, out of control, massive stage', depicting various paraphernalia and backdrops from tours gone by – film ready and prepared to shoot. 'Action!'

Disc One

'**The Ecstasy of Gold**' (2:02), '**Creeping Death**' (6:20), '**For Whom the Bell Tolls**' (4:40), '**Fuel**' (3:58), '**Ride the Lightning**' (6:55), '**One**' (8:25), '**The Memory Remains**' (5:43), '**Wherever I May Roam**' (6:19)

Disc Two

'**Cyanide**' (7:02)

A first live album outing for this high-octane *Death Magnetic* track and the crowd get behind the band, chanting with the usual enthusiasm across the intro riffs. The drums sound immense throughout, especially the double kick in the chorus sections.

'**...And Justice for All**' (9:18), '**Master of Puppets**' (8:26), '**Battery**' (5:14), '**Nothing Else Matters**' (7:22), '**Enter Sandman**' (6:22), '**Hit the Lights**' (4:40)

'Orion' (8:27)
New version recorded live during rehearsal sessions.

Hardwired...To Self-Destruct (2016)

Personnel:
Kirk Hammett: guitars
James Hetfield: guitars, vocals
Robert Trujillo: bass
Lars Ulrich: drums
Recorded at: HQ, San Rafael, California, between May 2015 and August 2016 and February and March 2012 ('Ronnie Rising Medley', 'When a Blind Man Cries'), May 2008 ('Remember Tomorrow'), live at Rasputin Music, Berkeley, CA on 16 April 2016 ('Helpless', 'Hit the Lights', 'The Four Horsemen', 'Ride the Lightning', 'Fade to Black, 'Jump in the Fire', 'For Whom The Bell Tolls', 'Creeping Death' and 'Metal Militia') and live at U.S. Bank Stadium, Minneapolis, MN on 20 August 2016 ('Hardwired').
Producer: Greg Fidelman with Hetfield and Ulrich
Release date: 18 November 2016
Chart placings: US: 1, UK: 2
Label: Blackened Recordings

By now, new challenges seem to come ten a dime for Metallica – but the end of 2013 brought one which few other bands can claim to have accomplished. On 8 December, they played an exclusive gig for competition winners and research scientists at the Carlini Base on the South Shetland Islands of Antarctica, making them the first band in rock and roll history to play shows across all seven continents in one year.

Thankfully, things got a little warmer come the new year with a string of 'Metallica By Request' concerts, launching in Bogota, Columbia and running until 9 August in Quebec. An interesting premise – fans voted online for their favourite tracks, with the band choosing one for themselves too.

In between taking requests across the world, they also made an appearance at Worthy Farm, in Pilton, UK – AKA the 'Glastonbury Festival' – another first for them and with hits like 'Enter Sandman', 'Nothing Else Matters' and 'Sad but True' doing nothing to harm their growing global appeal.

Summer dates and one-off shows were then peppered around recording sessions at Metallica HQ for the next long player in the making – including headline slots at both the Leeds and Reading UK festivals. This time, *Through the Never* producer Greg Fidelman was drafted in to oversee production duties and what follows is a practical extension of *Death Magnetic* before it. The fuller, fatter sound returns – not so much Bob Rock as Bob Rocks this time out – and there's a commercial aspect to the melodies that's been lacking since *Load*.

Lars shines out in 'Now That We're Dead' (track three) with some killer tom work in the intro and it's Hetfield's turn with his vocals in 'Halo on Fire' (track six). From mellow crooning, with a great tune, to the screaming in the chorus, it's an impressive range and shows his flexibility – for a growler, anyway.

The album ends with what I often hear is a fan favourite – the monstrous 'Spit Out the Bone' (track 12). It's not difficult to understand why it's so championed - a great end to the set and just as its title suggests, listeners feel like they've been well and truly gobbled up, stripped of any form of life and discarded without a care – 'No Remorse'.

The striking album artwork depicts a grotesque combined band member headshot from Turner Duckworth and Herring and Herring on the front, along with the familiar lightning band logo with an almost flatline cross through it – as does the album title below. Inside, along with full lyrics, the individual hellish headshots feature throughout.

Including five single releases, their quest for world domination seemingly continued – would they 'self-destruct' or destroy the airwaves?

'Hardwired' (3:09)

The death continues to be magnetised here as things kick off and we're away on a furious start. A maelstrom of snare drum and guitar stabs pair with a sawing riff underneath before we face a 'Battery' rampage. It's not long before the chorus comes blasting in, and my, they ain't holding back – 'we're so f*cked, shit outta luck – hardwired to self-destruct'. A triumphant Hetfield 'go!' then signals it all again. Kirk gets his obligatory (now) first song solo from 1:53; then Lars drives out of the last verse with his double kick pedals back into the battery of the end.

The album's lead single, released exactly three months before the album – 18 August 2016. It sent them to the top of the *Billboard* rock chart but only managed a criminal 186 in the UK.

'Atlas, Rise!' (6:28)

The drums drive the intro here, finishing with a great run around the kit and into a *Kill 'Em All* riff. Hetfield's vocal delivery, especially in the second half of the verses where he double speeds the phrasing, is right on point – rhythmically tight with the guitars: 'save-the-earth-and-claim-per-fection, deem-the-mass-and-blame-re-jection'.

The drums then take over again, driving the chorus along. There's a great lead guitar hang at 2:06 as the second verse kicks in – almost missable to the untrained ear, but a nod to those sonic sensibilities they've always possessed. The second chorus is double the length and as Hetfield screams out the final 'rise!', they break into an extended riffing passage until Kirk comes screaming in with the lead: 'Die as you suffer in vain, own all the grief and the pain. Die as you hold up the skies'. It sounds like something off *Ride the Lightning* in these passages, until, at 4:51, the modern-day verse kicks back in.

The third single (great choice) release – 31 October 2016. Topping the rock chart in the US but failing to chart anywhere in the UK. My favourite track on the album due to Hetfield's phrasing in the verses and that triumphant-sounding chorus.

'Now That We're Dead' (6:59)

From some studio amp feedback comes a grumbling riff, but it's the tom work that takes the interest in the intro here – sounding fat and wet (just the way Lars likes them). The recurring 'may it be' phrase is a criminal hook, burying deep into the subconscious – the listener expects it, wants it, needs it. Then when the title track lyric comes back in after the half-time riffing, it's as satisfying as anything they've ever recorded. The snare drum builds to a frenzy at 4:18, introducing a Kirk solo, then it breaks down, Fatty Tom taking over amidst more amplified angst, careering into the final chorus. Quite the celebration of suicide: 'When we're seduced, then may it be, that we not deviate our cause. Now that we're dead, my dear, we can be together, we can live forever. Return to ashes, shed this skin, beyond the black, we rise again'.

The fourth single release (another inspired choice) – 18 April 2017. It hit number two back home but failed to chart again in the UK.

'Moth Into Flame' (5:50)

Ride the Lightning raises its shocking head at the start again here, then Hetfield takes over – phrasing impeccable once more, leaving spaces between the riff – riding them like a black surfer. When the bridge kicks in at 1:02, the pace quickens dramatically. On the subsequent 'WorldWired' tour, this was accentuated brilliantly when played live by flumes of flames erupting from the stage between Lars and the rest of the gang – a health and safety nightmare but some spectacle! Kirk gets two solo spots here (making up for lost time), as a recurring refrain in the choruses, then later as the end of the track nears.

The second single, released – again ahead of the album – on 26 September. A US chart number five, but again failed to chart in the UK.

'Dream No More' (6:29)

The sonic experimentation resumes with a double-tracked Hetfield vocal that is striking in its snakelike, drawn-out delivery. It's one of the notable departures since the Bob Rock, radio-friendly days of the *Black Album* and *Load*s. This continues into the choruses – 'Cthulhu, awaken'. If ever that nod to *Ride the Lightning* was present, it's here my friends.

There's an exquisite moment of silence at 4:08, in which Hetfield appears to draw a breath, then Kirk takes over and the real 'Ktulu' is released – a hark back to those early days with Cliff.

'Halo on Fire' (8:15)

The main chorus riff features heavily in the intro here until Lars unleashes the snare drum, and the mood settles with some clean guitar and bass. Hetfield returns as the crooner with a high tone, but his rage soon boils over as he screams into the bridge section. A little lead guitar announces verse two and after the second chorus, the pace picks up into a driving riff over lead and drum flourishes. This section comes to the fore from 4:50, morphing into an almost separate song and at 5:49, after another clean guitar passage, a new song truly takes hold. 'Hello darkness/say goodbye' – marching to the end. A brilliant concept flawlessly executed.

'Confusion' (6:43)

Another trilogy looks to be finalised here – a tale of war. Bookending the themes of 'Disposable Heroes' and 'One' before it, this time focussing on the lasting after-effects of a shell-shocked veteran trying to return to normal life: 'War is never done, rub the patch and battle on. Make it go away, please make it go away'.

The bullet-like snare and guitar stabs of the intro bring the arena of warfare vividly to life, then a savage riff, before a spacey/lazy section, introduces verse one. A slight time signature change then brings in the 'confusion' of the chorus: 'My life.../the war that never ends'.

The snare bullets fire at the 'father please come home' section and at 4:27, the guitar riff is panned to the left, with drums pounding on the right – stabs of rhythm guitar coursing through the middle as the end section kicks in, leading to a Kirk solo. More bullets seal our fate as they rock out into the final chorus.

'ManUNkind' (6:55) (Hetfield/Ulrich/Trujillo)

Trujillo's sole writing credit on the album and he comes to the fore with the melodic bassline of the intro. At 45 seconds, the heaviness soon bleeds into a swingy riff, then bursts into a '2 X 4', *Load*-sounding section. Lars utilises an off-beat snare drum in the verses and the swinging riff rings out effectively over Hetfield's hanging 'UNkind' phrasing.

A new riff then suddenly appears off the back of chorus two, leading into a new section akin to the arrangement of 'Halo on Fire'. Kirk screams out relentlessly over the mid part of this passage until the '2 X 4' riff returns us full circle and brings in a final verse/chorus cycle.

'Here Comes Revenge' (7:17)

Some demonic-sounding lead guitar howls over the intro – setting the scene for this tale of manic, spiralling bitterness. After a shifting riff, a lead motif rings out over what will turn out to become the bridge sections. There's a great echoey effect on the bass and Lars' tom drums in the verse sections – some neat tom runs too – alongside some clean-sounding guitar. The second half of the verse then picks up pace and Lars announces the chorus with a full snare fill. Kirk takes over from 4:51, battling against the shifting rhythm guitar towards the final chorus and a jamlike final passage, with returning howling lead guitar – a swirling mist of fog/amp feedback to finish.

'Am I Savage?' (6:30)

More clean guitar, bass and drums feature in the intro before the heaviness engulfs to kick off the main riff. A snakelike, groovy riff precedes the chorus, pairing well with the animalistic lyrical theme – 'arching back, shape-shift derange'.

A sudden dead stop at 4:10 brings in a new evil-sounding riff and a Kirk solo, then another quick moment of silence heralds the final verse – Hetfield laughing us out to a stop.

'Murder One' (5:45)

Clean and heavy guitar duel during the intro before Lars pulls away with cymbals and snare into the main riff of this ode to Motorhead's Lemmy – the man, the myth, the sound. The track's title refers to the nickname of the frontman's famous amp – the Marshall Super Bass 100W – but the lyrics are littered with tributes to Lemmy himself: 'Aces wild, aces high, all the aces, aces 'til you die'.

Kirk pays personal tribute from 4:12 with a piercing solo, then rocks into the final chorus with the rest of them.

'Spit Out the Bone' (7:09)

As is often Metallica's want, they see out the album with a slice of superfast thrash. The attack is instantaneous, but Lars steers the course from just 25 seconds with a constant kick drum beat and snare drum fills, guitar riffs pummelling along with the rolls.

The verses are angry and played with precision, just like the *Kill 'Em All* days. At the end of the second chorus, after Hetfield scornfully 'spits' out the lyric, the hi-hat counts in a new riff with some distorted bass, and they career off into an extended instrumental section – Kirk relishing his final lead duties. At times, these last two minutes sound like a medley of all their sounds from previous albums – a Metallica melting pot. Finally, Kirk takes the wheel to hurtle into a final chorus and eventual silence.

The final single from the album released as a 'radio edit' on 14 November 2017. Reaching number four in the US, but yes, you've guessed it, failing to chart in the UK.

The track also featured in the WWE 2K19 video game as part of its soundtrack.

Bonus Tracks as featured on the Deluxe Edition release

'Lords of Summer' (7:10) (Hetfield/Ulrich/Trujillo)

This track was originally released as a stand-alone single in 2014 and will be considered later on in the book, but this version was re-recorded as part of the main *Hardwired* album sessions. With a slightly shorter intro – vocals enter at 1:11 – and a shorter lead guitar break, it's an 'almost' single, single version if you like.

'Ronnie Rising Medley' (9:03) (Blackmore/Dio/Powell)

Includes excerpts of 'A Light in the Black', 'Tarot Woman' and 'Stargazer', originally released by Rainbow on the 1976 *Rising* album and 'Kill the King', originally released by Rainbow on the 1978 *Long Live Rock 'n' Roll* album. Recorded for the Ronnie James Dio tribute album *This Is Your Life* in 2014. We only get a very quick blast of 'A Light in the Black' here – 33 seconds – then we're straight into the main riff of 'Tarot Woman', minus the original spacey intro, although Kirk does do a fine job of recreating some of the atmospheric mood. Lars then slows things down to bridge into a short passage of 'Stargazer', holding back a little on the original percussive intro. From 4:19, over a cry of 'now where do we go', Kirk unleashes the meat of this track – namely a full pelt version of 'Kill the King'. It's a very faithful rendition, featuring all the gusto of the original, plus no end of Kirk's lead playing. We're treated to a final few rounds of 'A Light in the Black' again to finish things off for good measure. Another medley job well done.

'When a Blind Man Cries' (4:35) (Blackmore/Gillan/Glover/Lord/Paice)

Originally released by Deep Purple as a B-side to the 1972 'Never Before' single. Recorded for the Deep Purple tribute album *Re-Machined* in 2012.
A hi-hat count-in adds to the song's authentic nature – mimicking the original to a T – and when Hetfield begins to sing, it's like the perfect echo of Ian Gillan's phrasing. The vocals are shiny and bright, as is Kirk's lead guitar at 1:21 – lazy, wistful and mourning. The heaviness is finally cranked up from 3:09, leading the track out in typical Metallica fashion, most unlike the original.

'Remember Tomorrow' (5:50) (Harris/Di'Anno)

Originally released by Iron Maiden on the 1980 *Iron Maiden* album. Recorded for the Iron Maiden tribute album *Maiden Heaven* in 2008.
With a little artistic integrity, a hybrid version of the original main chorus riff kicks things off here, before settling into a steady, Trujillo-flavoured take on the verse section – complete with clean guitar too. However, Metallica match Maiden stride-for-stride at 2:37 when the powerful instrumental passage takes hold. It's like a battle through the ages, until the calmness returns briefly at 3:49, replete with some soulful Kirk lead, before erupting with 'fire' to take us neatly to the end and back to that initial 'hybrid' riff.

'Helpless' (3:08), 'Hit the Lights' (4:07), 'The Four Horsemen' (5:19), 'Ride the Lightning' (6:56), 'Fade to Black' (7:24), 'Jump in the Fire' (5:13), 'For Whom the Bell Tolls' (4:32), 'Creeping Death' (6:43), 'Metal Militia' (6:07)

'Hardwired' (3:30)

The first official live outing release for this track, which is pretty much a straight album to live show version, double-stamped by Hetfield boasting to the crowd at the end: 'hardwired for you baby – first time live, I love it'. A nice collector's edition, for sure.

S&M2 (2020)

Personnel:
Kirk Hammett: guitars
James Hetfield: guitars, vocals
Robert Trujillo: bass
Lars Ulrich: drums
Scott Pingel: bass solo on '(Anesthesia) – Pulling Teeth'.
Avi Vinocur: additional vocals on 'All Within My Hands'.
Edwin Outwater: conductor and musical director
Nadya Tichman (concertmaster), Jeremy Constant, Mariko Smiley, Melissa
Kleinbart, Sarn Oliver, Naomi Kazama Hull, Victor Romasevich, Yun Chu, Yukika
Kurakata and Katie Kadarauch: first violinists
Jessie Fellows, Polina Sedukh, David Chernyavsky, Raushan Akhmedyarova,
Chen Zhao, Adam Smyla, Sarah Knutson and Yuna Lee: second violinists
Yun Jie Liu, John Schoening, Christina King, Gina Cooper, David Gaudry,
Matthew Young, David Kim and Nanci Severance: violas
Amos Yang, Margaret Tait, Jill Rachuy Brindel, Stephen Tramontozzi, Shu-Yi Pai,
Richard Andaya, Miriam Perkoff and Adelle-Akiko Kearns: cellos
Scott Pingel, Daniel G. Smith, S. Mark Wright, Charles, Chandler, Chris Gilbert
and William Ritchen: basses
Robin McKee, Linda Lukas and Catherine Payne: flutes
James Button, Pamela Smith and Russ deLuna: oboes
Luis Baez, David Neuman and Jerome Simas: clarinets
Stephen Paulson, Rob Weir and Steven Braunstein: bassoons
Robert Ward, Jonathan Ring, Bruce Roberts, Daniel Hawkins, Chris Cooper,
Joshua Paulus and Jeff Garza: horns
Aaron Schuman, Joseph Brown, Robert Giambruno and John Freeman: trumpets
Timothy Higgins, Nick Platoff, John Engelkes and Jeff Budin: trombones
Jeffrey Anderson: tuba
Edward Stephen: timpani
Jacob Nissly, James Lee Wyatt III, Tom Hemphill and Robert Klieger: percussion
Douglas Rioth: harp
Marc Shapiro: keyboard
Recorded live at: The Chase Center, San Francisco, California on 6 and 8
September 2019, using the Music Mix Mobile M3
Producer: Greg Fidelman with Hetfield and Ulrich
Release date: 28 August 2020
Chart placings: US: 1, UK: 2
Label: Blackened Recordings

The 'WorldWired' tour actually kicked off on 20 August 2016 at the US Bank
Stadium in Minneapolis and ran right through to 25 August 2019, finishing with
a show in Mannheim, Germany. En route, having realised it had been 20 years
since the original *S&M* project, and seeing as they'd been invited to open the

new Chase Center in San Francisco, the germ of the idea for a follow-up was planted. With the sad passing of Michael Kamen in 2003, new reworkings were left in the capable hands of San Francisco Symphony's Musical Director Michael Tilson Thomas, though many of the original arrangements were also included in the two nights of performances on 6 and 8 September 2019.

The explosive album artwork sets it apart from its more conservative predecessor, featuring the classic lightning 'M' smashing through what looks like a cello – the instrument's markings cleverly making up the 'S' and '2' on either side of it. The gatefold cover features live shots of the performance, and the inlay has detailed notes from both Tilson Thomas and conductor Edwin Outwater, along with more performance photography from long-time snapper Anton Corbijn.

Disc One
'The Ecstasy of Gold' (2:41)
It doesn't feel like it's been 20 years since we first settled down to the original *S&M*, but as the crowd hums along to the opening bars and becomes rapturous again as their heroes take to the stage, it seems like only yesterday.

'The Call of Ktulu' (9:14)
Just like part one – 'Ktulu' is the first track proper once more – a nice touch. The roar from the crowd again as it really kicks into life is thoroughly invigorating. It also fits this project perfectly again, with a symphonic quality that makes it 'the' absolute best opener.

'For Whom the Bell Tolls' (4:37)
Not 'Puppets', not 'Creeping Death', not even anything from the *Black Album* next. We're thrown straight against the bells, and they fairly ring out. A show-stopping end-of-performance favourite placed at track two (not counting 'Ecstasy of Gold'). Outrageous behaviour.

'The Day That Never Comes' (8:27)
The orchestra do a fine job on the intro here and it's great to hear the newer songs given this treatment. This one soars, particularly during the faster end section, where the symphonic partnership embellishes it in all the right places.

'The Memory Remains' (5:42)
The crowd get back on side with a very 'Faithfull' version here. They're deafening, belting out the title, as well as singing the haunting chorus melody well into the end – accompanying the dying twinkles of the orchestra.

'Confusion' (6:41)
A brace of the really brand new comes next, this first one lending itself well to the musical partnership – adding even more drama and suspense to the

original composition. The crowd come to the fore once again during the intro and the horn section sounds suitably insane in the choruses.

'Moth Into Flame' (6:18)
The orchestra are strangely scarce in most of the verse sections, but it doesn't detract from the power of the performance. They resurface nicely in the final one and build effectively with the band towards the end section.

'The Outlaw Torn' (10:03)
After two new tracks, we get two S&M stalwarts. The orchestra get this off to a start and the melodies over the driving riff complement it well. They then leave lots of space around the solos at the end as the track drives to its conclusion.

'No Leaf Clover' (5:30)
An old friend returns – one of the 'new' tracks that featured on the original S&M project. The effects on Hetfield's vocals in the pre-chorus sections are disappointingly absent, however – which is a shame – a missed trick. However, the guitars really crunch in the final passage as we come to the final song before the interval...

'Halo on Fire' (8:17)
Broodingly brilliant, the orchestra lends a disturbing air to the verse sections and Hetfield plunges the depths of his vocal range in the choruses – screaming out into them. The Symphony and crowd burst together with life towards the end in a celebration of music and metal.

Disc Two
'Intro to Scythian Suite' (5:16)
Lars takes the mic after the interval to warmly welcome the Metallica Club members for attending, including fans from Poland, Germany, Mexico, Denmark and Brazil, among others – no UK name-drops, I might add! He then thanks conductor Edwin Outwater before introducing the Symphony's Musical Director Michael Tilson Thomas, who goes on to introduce the next track, namely Prokofiev's dark piece about the tribal, horse-loving Scythians – metal and classical fusing together, what could possibly go wrong?

'Scythian Suite, Opus 20 II' (3:39) (Prokofiev)
'The Dance of the Ecstatic Spirits of the Night' is duly reeled off by the Symphony – it's epic and grandiose and Tilson Thomas was right – it suits the theme of the evening and Metallica's music perfectly.

'Intro to The Iron Foundry' (1:03)
Tilson Thomas goes on to introduce the next track and this really is a fusion. The power of the machine – accompanied by none other than the band themselves!

'The Iron Foundry, Opus 19' (4:16) (Mosolov)
As the timpani starts to roll – it's not long before Lars and the guitars join in. It's stomping mayhem – not unlike some of the band's own instrumental offerings. The horns kick in to add to the drama and it's a continuing loop of mayhem until ...

'The Unforgiven III' (8:19)
A moment of hush lulls across the audience and the anticipation is audible as Hetfield takes the centre spot for a wonderful rendition. Not a single electric guitar can be heard and he owns that stage. There's pure emotion oozing out of him throughout – straining in parts, but that only adds to the performance. The 'forgive' me sections hold almost as much power as the original version – the crooner done good.

'All Within My Hands' (6:14)
The only *St. Anger* offering this night, which gets a similar, more acoustic treatment and really shows its melodic, non-aggressive nature. What Metallica 'Unplugged' might sound like. It's good, but not 'that' good.

'(Anesthesia) – Pulling Teeth' (7:28)
A classical bass tribute to Cliff is a beautiful moment – he's absolutely there and with Lars again too. A surprising, yet inspired choice and the Scott Pingel playing is exceptional – I'm sure he would approve.

'Wherever I May Roam' (6:32)
Starting a 'final five' gig run that you'd be hard pushed to better – we'll forgive Hetfield for getting the words wrong just before the first chorus too.

'One' (9:24)
A dramatic intro that could (and should have) go(ne) on forever sets up a clean guitar sound that is heartbreakingly beautiful – I mean, really! What's clever here is how the beauty of the first stages morphs so cuttingly into the more harrowing, second section. There's a flurry of strings, horns and bells as the horror of Kirk's solo comes screaming in.

'Master of Puppets' (8:30)
Another full version – saving the best till almost last. The strings in the intro bring this monster fully to life and the energy is apparent.

The crowd sing out Kirk's timeless solo in majestic fashion, then the orchestra underpin the heaviness of the 'Master! Master!' section in the best way, paving the way for Kirk's second bite at his cherry' – and my, does he fly!

'Nothing Else Matters' (6:40)
The crowd don't know what's coming at the start here and neither do we –

but we do, kinda, don't we? THE ballad – the best orchestra accompaniment, and Kirk's solo is absolutely spot on.

'Enter Sandman' (8:46)
The crowd really do sound like they know what's coming at the start here, but now we all do too. Hetfield restrains the expletives in the second half of the first verse for once and Kirk's solo sounds even angrier. Later, we get the ends of our sanities slightly frayed as the outro lingers – a wonderful little touch – the teases.

72 Seasons (2023)

Personnel:
Kirk Hammett: guitars
James Hetfield: guitars, vocals
Robert Trujillo: bass
Lars Ulrich: drums
Recorded at: HQ, San Rafael, California, between March 2021 and November 2022
Producer: Greg Fidelman with Hetfield and Ulrich
Release date: 14 April 2023
Chart placings: US: 2, UK: 1
Label: Blackened Recordings

Riding the crest of a wave from their *S&M2* success, the band intended to head off back to Australia and New Zealand for a number of shows towards the end of 2019. Unfortunately, however, all eight shows had to be cancelled as Hetfield entered another round of rehab due to continuing difficulties with addiction. A heartfelt statement from the band read: 'As most of you probably know, our brother James has been struggling with addiction on and off for many years. He has now had to re-enter a treatment program to work on his recovery again'.

As the Covid-19 pandemic crippled the globe in 2020, further planned shows were cancelled, resulting in just a handful of appearances, namely a Metallica crew bubble show at the Gunlach Bundschu winery in Sonoma, California, which was later beamed out to drive-in movie theatres across the States, a spot on the Howard Stern show, filmed at the band's HQ on 12 August and an online benefit gig, also filmed at HQ on 14 November, featuring an acoustic first set including a newly 'covid' arranged version of 'Blackened', 'Creeping Death' and 'Now That We're Dead' among others.

The following year proved more optimistic, heralding two major milestones in the band's career. Firstly their own 40th anniversary and secondly, the 30th birthday of the *Black Album*.
A deluxe remastered box set of the latter and a collaborative *Blacklist* project featuring 53 different artists covering cuts from the album, took care of initial celebrations for both occasions.

The main event took place at the end of the year, with two dates back at San Francisco's Chase Center on 17 and 19 December, featuring at least one track from each studio album in chronological order, oldest to newest on the first night, then in reverse order on the second.

With covid now a somewhat manageable beast and worldwide travel back on the cards, 2022 saw the band venture to South America and across Europe before dropping the new album announcement bomb in November.

Hetfield surmised the concept of *72 Seasons* on the official Metallica website as:

The first 18 years of our lives that form our true or false selves. The concept that we were told 'who we are' by our parents. A possible pigeon-holing around what kind of personality we are. I think the most interesting part of this is the continued study of those core beliefs and how it affects our perception of the world today. Much of our adult life experience is a re-enactment or reaction to these childhood experiences. Prisoners of childhood or breaking free of those bondages we carry.

Confused? We will be...

Taking a mammoth 18 months to record, the longest timeframe for any of their previous 11 studio outputs, is this then a tortured tale of a soul from birth to young adult – a metal concept album, as Hetfield suggests? Or the more usual demonic depictions of gothic gods, with satanic riffs and rumbling rhythms? A little of both it seems on closer inspection.

The album artwork is a striking departure itself; various burnt-out paraphernalia, all black of course (guitar/soft toys/alarm clock/sunglasses), lie strewn across the floor below a baby's cot with its centre wooden slats seemingly blown apart – all against a bright yellow backdrop. The famous lightning M is featured neatly in the top right corner. An easy eye-catcher in the record racks for sure. The cardboard CD inlay folds out to show *Time Magazine* photographer Lee Jeffries' mugshot portraits of the four band members, backed with photos of more charred furniture and accessories. It's simple, it's slick and it's also somewhat disturbing.

As for the music on offer, after what might have sounded a little constrained and rigid at times with the previous studio album *Hardwired* – as if they were following some kind of formula, akin to the longer, two, often three-in-one song tricks heard in the earlier albums – here it sounds free of any kind of restrictions. Like improvised jam sessions, ideas sound as if they've been thrown around the rehearsal room floor, left to evolve by their own devices, before being committed to tape and yet the wait is worth it. This is a welcome collection for any long-time, fully invested fan.

The title track is like a perfectly wrapped gift that just keeps on giving. A reward for sticking with them and staying loyal for so long. In fact, the first five tracks all deliver the Metallica goods.

The commercialism of 'Lux Æterna' (track six) then divides the album almost in half - the first single release that seems to belie the full concept and overall theme of the album.

And therein lies the small problem when considering that concept across the whole package – it just doesn't quite work. The hints are too few, too sparing for it to be fully realised across the entire album.

What does work, however, is its material. Bursting with new life, a re-energised, youthful exuberance and complete and utter confidence. The studio break clearly did them good and surely paves the way for more of the same and a few more surprises in years to come too.

The production is similar, of course, this is the sound of *Hardwired* and similar to *Death Magnetic*, punchy and fat, concise and compact. In fact, what follows sounds, in parts, like an extension of the self-destruction that came before it. Like *Load* and *Reload*, *Hardwired* and this album fit well together – solid bedfellows. The only difference is the single concept this time out and it's a hard one to try and get your head around. With themes of suicide, witchcraft, drug abuse and psychosis, it's difficult to imagine they could all be experienced by anyone before the tender age of 18 – as the overall album concept supposedly suggests. Then again, this is a world quite like no other, with trappings that many would find hard to resist. Their first UK number one album since 2008's *Death Magnetic* - does this ambitious concept translate well through the familiar wall and barrage of guitars and drums? We've only got 72 Seasons to find out ...

'72 Seasons' (7:39) (Hetfield/Ulrich/Hammett)

Track one and it's the title track. We're in, and we're in big and bold as brass.

The intro sounds just like 'Frantic' from *St. Anger*, but you can put those ear defenders down – this is no enforced racket. Trujillo rumbles along with Lars' double-speed hi-hats before some evil guitar stabs announce a grinding riff, then a quick one-two into a 'Battery' sounding death march. As the verses settle, a main riff fully takes hold and it sounds like they've been playing it for years. It's 1:36 before we get a Hetfield vocal and boy does he make every syllable count, driving in time with Lars' snare roll: 'fee-ding-on-the-wrath-of-man'. He sounds angry and with a point to prove. Well, it has been nearly six-and-a-half years since their last recorded output proper.

The bridge section features some impressive Lars tom pounding over a more familiar-sounding chugging riff, until the 'wrath of man' phrase is repeated effectively over the chorus sections, which break quickly, almost surprisingly out of the stomp before it. Then, as if to catch us off guard again, out of a double-length snare drum roll, Kirk comes lurching out of the depths with a sinister-sounding lead break, mimicking the main riff towards its end. That's the first three minutes taken care of.

A breakdown at 4:16 allows us some brief respite, but only brief; soon enough, a new section is introduced featuring some demonic backing vocals ('piercing *through*/cut in *two*') and a second lead break. As we approach the end, at 5:58, all band members unleash hell, pounding relentlessly into a final verse/bridge/chorus run.

Overall, there's little clue in the lyrics to the concept: 'staring into black light, dominating birthright... choking on the stage fright'. This sounds more like the familiar ode to a disturbed and troubled individual – one battling many demons at once – rather apt as usual.

A slight niggle here is the way Hetfield seems to stumble out the words of the title at the end of the chorus sections. '72 seasons' always seems rushed – under-rehearsed almost. It would sound better to this reviewer if he'd spat them out in a more staccato style – similar to the way he does the 'you-know-it's-sad-but-true(s)' on the *Black Album*. He does do it once, at the very end, in time with Lars' snare roll, but with different lyrics: 'fee-ding-on-the-wrath-of man' again. But by then, it's too late – '72 seasons gone' ...

The fourth and final single release from the album, dropping on 30 March 2023.

'Shadows Follow' (6:12)

If it wasn't for the brief silence at the end of the previous track and the stop/start nature of the rather disjointed intro here – when the first verse kicks in, you can forgive yourself for thinking it's the same track – you can practically sing the '72 Seasons' verse lyrics over it.

That comes to an end during the unsettling bridge/chorus sections, however: 'seething, breathing, nightmares grow'.

A half-time section, featuring some on-point snare and tom drum fills, takes over at 2:51, leading into another bridge section with a duelling guitar solo before going into an extended lead break.

A huge nod to Lars, who plays a massive role in the dynamics of this track, most notably in his snare drum fills, then the nine sharp kick and cymbal stabs in the chorus sections: 'on-I-run-still-my-shadows-follow!'

'Screaming Suicide' (5:30) (Hetfield/Ulrich/Trujillo)

A wah-wah intro bleeds brilliantly into a hooky riff during the intro, before the first verse kicks off and motors along nicely – it's a breakneck start to the album with three high-octane tracks in a row.

Hetfield utilises his metal rap technique during the verses; the phrasing is fast, and its staccato nature bleeds effectively into a lazy bridge with lazier drums before the chorus.

The guitars and drums then unite, before driving home the chorus lyrics with an evil-sounding, savage intention: 'keep-me-in-side, my name is suicide'. The riff then pummels on into a solo section – Kirk is having a field day on this album.

The lyrics on this track tell a familiar tale, one of the desperation of suicidal intentions and the battling of demons in the mind. There is a glint of hope in this one, however. 'Don't ever speak my name, remember you're to blame', then later 'and now you speak my name, you've given back the blame. Keep-me-deep-in-side-don't-you keep me inside. Screaming suicide'. Hetfield holds onto the last 'suicide' over Lars' snare roll with real aplomb, before banishing the unwanted devil for good: 'I'm no longer needed here, now you've faced your biggest fear'. It appears that for once, the protagonist in this particular horror story comes out on top.

The second single release from the album – 19 January 2023 – climbing to number 32 on the *Billboard* Hot Rock & Alternative Songs chart. My favourite track on the album due to its lyrical cleverness and the way the guitars and drums brutally sledgehammer into the 'keep-me-in-side' sections.

'Sleepwalk My Life Away' (6:56) (Hetfield/Ulrich/Trujillo)

Trujillo's writing credit is brought to the fore during the intro here, grinding along perfectly with Lars' double-time tom fills. After a few rounds, a main riff motif joins in until they all come in together to launch the full verse at 1:14.

There's a distinct *Black Album*, 'Of Wolf and Man' steer to the lyrics here: 'Stagger on through the fog in the midnight sun. Shouting out the shapes of the nameless one'.

An impressive, unexpected dead stop at 3:51 ushers in an extended Kirk solo section – he's really getting to flex his muscles this time out. Then from 4:53, that improvised, almost experimental feel comes back into play. These are long songs, but they don't seem to follow any specific, set formula. They are allowed to grow and mature, almost in front of our own ears. It's a refreshing and quite different sound for Metallica. We even get some studio floor mumblings at the end from Lars – 'that was good, right?'

'You Must Burn!' (7:03) (Hetfield/Ulrich/Trujillo)

From the brand new to the classic sounding; when the main riff kicks in here from just 25 seconds in, it sounds like we're back in the realms of *Puppetz*, with evil-sounding guitars and a scything, swinging drum pattern. The lyrics are a hark back to those 'Phantom Lord' and 'Leper Messiah' days, too: 'in the name of hell, henchmen to conspire. Black figures loom as a dark desire'.

At 3:14, Lars takes full control of the song, his snare drum stabs forcing the track into a slightly new direction, one which later submerses Hetfield into a further world of horror, almost moaning out the lyrics: 'in the heat of the night, in the moon's shining light, feed the appetite'.

Kirk then takes the 'lead' into a final chorus: 'question yourself, you may learn. You are the witch you must burn'.

'Lux Æterna' (3:22)

A slice of pure radio rock, at odds with most of the other content on the album. The shortest track on offer here, but that does nothing to dull its impact.

The energy is apparent from the offset, with Lars treading his infamous double kick pedals all over the introductory riff passages – then again over the chorus sections.

A manic Kirk solo comes reeling off the back of a brief 'Four Horsemen'-like breakdown, which then neatly dovetails us back into a final verse/chorus run.

The track's title bears little resemblance to the overall lyrical theme on offer here. This is no music for a Catholic Requiem – more like the mandate of a power-crazed adrenaline junkie. 'Full speed or nothing'.

This was the first single to drop from the album on 28 November 2022. It failed to dent the main *Billboard* chart, but it hit the number one spot on the Hot Mainstream Rock Tracks chart in the US.

'Crown of Barbed Wire' (5:49) (Hetfield/Ulrich/Hammett)

Out of some pummelling drums and guitar bleeds a main riff, again more commercial sounding, which wouldn't seem out of place on a mainstream rock radio show. The lyrics are not so commercial, however; there's some real Christ-like imagery on offer in the verse sections here – 'fist tight, it stains conviction. Drips down to bloodshot eyes. It crushes down what is real. Deep crimson blots the skies'. But we are all brainwashed disciples here, aren't we?

During the bridge, Hetfield further paves the way for his unfortunate anti-hero: 'This rusted empire I own, bleed as I rust on this throne. Pierce. Me. With torment'. Then pleads with us over the chorus: 'so tight this crown'.

At 3:18, a new riff announces a shift in the song, moving it in a slightly new direction, with Kirk taking the lead once again. The drums then drive us back into a final bridge/chorus run. A neat arrangement where they show again that they aren't shy of throwing formulas to the fire and doing things their own way.

'Chasing Light' (6:45) (Hetfield/Ulrich/Hammett)

A scream of 'there's no light' from Hetfield opens things up here, before settling into a sledgehammer opening guitar and drum pattern. But at just 44 seconds, a classic-sounding riff kicks in, reminiscent of something from the early days – *Kill 'Em All* like in its ferocity. The coin is then flipped expertly as the measured verse hits home, revealing the new, downright experimental Metallica of the 2020s. The pace then quickens in the bridge sections, allowing the chorus to open up into a crowd sing-a-long section: 'chase that light, lean on me!'

Here finally, we get a shrouded glimpse of the main concept in the verse lyrics: 'lost his way through wicked streets, but he is someone's little boy. All the love a young one needs, thoughtless elders have destroyed'. The first 18 years of anyone's life are unquestionably the most influential. There will never be a more important phase in the development of a young mind, where core beliefs, values and impressions are absorbed and burned into the psyche. And if that young mind has been cruelly manipulated and distorted by the very people who are supposed to be guiding it, as the lyrics here suggest, what hope does it have? What hope do any of us have? It's maybe a little too late with it being track number eight, but at least it finally 'shines' more light on the ambitious concept theme.

Another shift change at 3:43 takes us in a completely new direction again and another lead break back into a final chorus, revealing that, although this new album often appears to tear up the Metallica rulebook at times, it also further underlines the band's appetite to push the 'standard' song format to its absolute limit – particularly in the closing stages here.

'If Darkness Had a Son' (6:36) (Hetfield/Ulrich/Hammett)

With a deafening thudding stomp, Lars 'kicks off' this track, soon adding a militaristic snare drum roll for good measure. As the guitars chime in, it's an incessant attack which doesn't let up until 1:05, a hypnotic, almost psychotic loop that seems to bury into your subconsciousness – hammered home by the repeated phrase of 'temptation' from 1:22.

'The Thing That Should Not Be' from the *Puppetz* album raises its ugly head again in the bridge section(s): 'the never-ending quenchless craving, the unforgiving misbehaving' – it's markedly similar in melody and structure. Kirk's extended lead break from 3:48 then takes us back down a familiar bridge/chorus run and Hetfield plays things out with another twist, emphasising the 'here I am(s)' to great effect.

Surely an autobiographical tale of the lead singer's battles over the years - 'if darkness had a son, here I am. Temptation is his father ... Temptation, - leave (Hetfield)/me be'.

The third – and rather surprising – single pick from the album, was released on 1 March 2023 and reached the number one spot on the *Billboard* Hot Trending Songs chart.

'Too Far Gone' (4:34)

After the literal 'darkness' of most of the album so far, a little light relief is shined on proceedings here – at least in regards to the music and structure of the piece. The lyrics continue in the same vein: 'I am desperation, need it so bad today. I am isolation, static and disarray'. The new rule book is notably brandished again, too, not least from 1:39 when we get an almost instant Kirk lead guitar break.

That aforementioned light relief comes into play at 2:33 when the track suddenly turns into what sounds almost like a pop song, with a commercial duelling guitar riff and some harmonised vocals: 'all away'. Another full Kirk lead follows, sitting neatly sandwiched between the more 'poppy' sections, rounding off the second shortest track from the album.

'Room of Mirrors' (5:34)

As this collection draws to its inevitable conclusion, the pace does not let up. There's a debut feel to the tempo here, particularly with the riff which introduces the first verse. The same can be said of the way Hetfield scoffs out the lyrics: 'in a mirrored room, all alone I stand, strip away the phantom fame'. He brings us back to the near present a little later with a cute name-drop to a *Death Magnetic* track, namely 'broken, beat, and scarred'.

Overall, it's a clear analysis of the trappings of fame and fortune: 'so I stand here before you, you might judge, you might just bury me'. I think we'll let the fans be the overall judge of that!

After a lead break from 2:43, a hooky lead guitar refrain is introduced at 3:36, driving us into a final bridge/chorus. This section lifts the track to another level for the final couple of minutes, with Lars' double kick pedals also joining the party. Some barely audible studio floor mumblings can be picked up at the very end – but you really have to listen hard, ear to speaker, volume to 11 – before turning the sound down quickly of course!

'Inamorata' (11:10)

The final track – and do they save the best 'til last? Well, it's certainly the longest. At just over 11 minutes, it's their longest studio album track so far. Longer than 'Ktulu' from *Lightning*, longer than 'Orion' from *Puppetz*, and even longer than the sprawling 'To Live is to Die' and title track from *Justice*. This is no instrumental either. It begins in this vein, however, and sounds like it could well have been in the initial writing stages – it's got that sort of feel to it.

A driving riff rumbles along effectively and it's not until the 1:13 mark that a Hetfield vocal invites us to join him at the party: 'welcome, won't you come inside. Meet the ghosts where I reside'. The cunning trick in the early part of this song is the way that the vocal melody over the second bridge section is completely different to that of the first. The shifting nature of the 'she waits, she waits' phrasing sets us up for something a little out of the ordinary again. After this, a lead break screams out over a cutting riff – and we're only 4:45 in so far. A breakdown to just the hi-hat and bass then allows Hetfield to really express his emotions – in that way only he can do – unleashing all that pent-up frustration in time with Lars' building snare drum rolls.

Lyrically this is no picnic. There are many woes encumbering the unfortunate protagonist in this particular tale: 'misery, she kills me. Oh, but I end this war. Misery, she fills me. Oh no, but she's not what I'm living'. Amen to that!

An almost poetic, at times majestic, duelling guitar lead pattern then takes centre stage for a while from 6:40, leading to the track's finale and a seemingly constant cycle of the misery, with a new hypnotic riff taking hold at 8:52 and later, more heartbreakingly pleading 'no no(s)' from Hetfield.

As the guitars eventually fade, we get a final nod of approval from Hetfield himself on the studio floor: 'that was the best one'. We think he's probably right.

Part Five: Through the Never and Beyond

Singles, EPs and Specials

Live at Wembley Stadium (1992)

Personnel:

Kirk Hammett: guitars

James Hetfield: guitars, vocals

Jason Newsted: bass

Lars Ulrich: drums

Recorded at: Wembley Stadium, London, on 20 April 1992, at the Freddie Mercury Tribute Concert

Mixed by: Flemming Rasmussen

Release date: 27 April 1992

Chart placings: did not chart

Label: Vertigo

If you'd have told the Metallica who first played at Radio City, Anaheim, California back in 1982, that they'd open up for Queen at Wembley Stadium just ten years later, they'd most probably have laughed you off the stage. But that's exactly what happened here as part of the concert commemorating the life and work of one Freddie Mercury. Sandwiched between US dates on the first leg of their colossal 'Wherever We May Roam' world tour – playing their most successful hit to date (and future hits) – it did no harm at all to their growing stature as the biggest heavy metal band in the world.

'Enter Sandman' (5:39)

Introduced by Queen's bass player John Deacon, it's a great start to any gig. Lars' toms in the intro sound bigger and fatter than ever and their sound fills the sell-out stadium for sure. Hetfield's vocals are strong and fierce.

'Sad but True' (5:30)

Pleasing the (Metallica) fans in the stadium by hitting track two of *the* album next. The live sound of the guitars is crunchy as hell and Kirk's little lead motif in the choruses shines through.

'Nothing Else Matters' (6:17)

The madness of the previous track bleeds straight into the plaintive picking and turns quite a few non-metallic heads in the stadium, no doubt. The rage of the final section is somewhat subdued, as seems Kirk's lead, but it's a decent rendition that most probably shifted another few hundred thousand copies of the album – a good day's work.

Hetfield would later take to the stage with Queen and Tony Iommi from Black Sabbath for a performance of 'Stone Cold Crazy' – another dream realised.

One (Live) (1994)

Personnel:
Kirk Hammett: guitars
James Hetfield: guitars, vocals
Jason Newsted: bass
Lars Ulrich: drums
Recorded at: One on One, Los Angeles, California from January to May 1988 ('One'), the Sports Arena, San Diego, California on 13 and 14 January 1992 ('One (Live)' and ('Whiplash (Live)') and the Seattle Coliseum, Seattle, Washington on 29 and 30 August 1989 ('For Whom the Bell Tolls (Live)' and 'Last Caress (Live)')
Producer: Metallica with Flemming Rasmussen ('One' and 'One (Edit)', not produced ('One (Demo)' and Hetfield & Ulrich (live tracks)
Release date: 11 April 1994
Chart placings: did not chart
Label: Vertigo

'One' (7:24)
The studio version from the album.

'One (Demo)' (7:03)
Recorded on Hetfield's four-track machine soon after it was written in early November 1987. No bass and unfinished lyrics – with Kirk supplying the second solo after only hearing the song the day before! A fascinating insight into the writing and recording process for fans.

'One (Live)' (10:27)
The *Live Shit* DVD performance.

'One (Edit)' (5:02)
The 'single' remix, as it were. A lone helicopter pans right to left at the start and we get a shortened intro going straight into verse one here. The backing vocals sound far more pronounced in the initial stages, and we don't get the second guitar solo. Fade at the end...

'Whiplash (Live)' (4:46)
The *Live Shit* DVD performance.

'For Whom the Bell Tolls (Live)' (5:50)
The *Live Shit* DVD performance.

'Last Caress (Live)' (2:25)
The *Live Shit* DVD performance.

Live In London: The Antipodean Tour Edition (1998)
Personnel:
Kirk Hammett: guitars
James Hetfield: guitars, vocals
Jason Newsted: bass
Lars Ulrich: drums
Recorded at: The Ministry of Sound, London, UK on 13 November 1997
Mixed by: James 'Jimbo' Barton
Release date: 2 March 1998
Chart placings: did not chart
Label: Vertigo

Taken from the start of the 'Blitzkrieg '97' tour, this recording is a snapshot of a very brief UK leg and three TV/radio appearances – four in two days in fact. As well as this Ministry of Sound appearance, they featured on *Top of the Pops* (on the same day!) and on Virgin Radio and the *TFI Friday* magazine TV programme the day after.

'Bleeding Me (Live)' (8:33)
The guitar sounds watery at the start and although Lars' snare drum is a little tinny at first, the toms soon join in the moistness as the first verse takes hold. Hetfield has the crowd on side during the bridge section and just before the final choruses, as the riff cranks up and Kirk solos over the double-timed end.

'Stone Cold Crazy (Live)' (3:32)
The final song before the encore of this show and the crowd are in fine voice again – helping Hetfield out with the first verse and belting out the track's title too! Complete with Hetfield expletives, of course, which he aims firmly at the crowd before they leave the stage.

'The Wait (Live)' (4:44)
The first encore song ('Puppets' would follow) and a cool hark back to those 'garage days' when Newsted – whose deft playing is pronounced over Kirk's exceptional solo – was just a Metalli-rookie. Hetfield's vocal is suitably angry.

'Damage, Inc. (Live)' (4:54)
Encore two and the final song. The energy is amazingly sustained – some feat after a show of thirteen other songs. Kirk's solo is once again spot on and the UK crowd sound like they go home very happy.

I Disappear (2000)
Personnel:
Kirk Hammett: guitars
James Hetfield: guitars, vocals

Jason Newsted: bass
Lars Ulrich: drums
Producer: Bob Rock with Hetfield and Ulrich
Release date: 26 June 2000
Chart placings: US: 76, UK: 35
Label: Hollywood Records

Recorded to order for the Tom Cruise *Mission: Impossible II* movie and although it was actually Limp Bizkit who released the official 'Theme From' track, this one did not come without its fair share of demons and eventual bad publicity. Prior to its release, a demo of the track started to appear on the US radio waves. The source? – a new internet-sharing programme named Napster. Cue a huge Metallica-backed lawsuit and Lars testifying before the US Senate Judiciary Committee. The furore did not go down well among some fans who found the juxtaposition of what their drumming idol used to do with his NWOBHM pals back in the 1980s: trading ripped-off cassettes of his favourite bands, not too dissimilar to the Napster ethos.

Along with Newsted's un-acrimonious leaving just a few months later, it all added up to a rather 'tricky' time for the band. Maybe that's where the real *St. Anger* later came from – and who'd want to share that after all ...

'I Disappear' (4:26)

A brain-drilling riff is initially panned to the left before the drums and rhythm join in. This is definitely a Metallica for a new millennium with shed loads of effects and samples on offer – an attack on the charts. It has a clear *Load*-like feel to it in stark contrast to the *St. Anger* aggression, which would follow in a few years' time.

It only just dented the US *Billboard* Hot 100 at a 'disappearing' number 76, but hit a more respectable number 35 in the UK chart.

'I Disappear (Instrumental)' (4:32)

The Unnamed Feeling EP (2004)

Personnel:
Kirk Hammett: guitars
James Hetfield: guitars, vocals
Bob Rock: bass: bass
Robert Trujillo: bass
Lars Ulrich: drums
Recorded at: HQ, San Rafael, California, between May 2002 and April 2003 ('The Unnamed Feeling'), Le Bataclan, Paris on 11 June 2003 ('The Four Horsemen (Live)', 'Damage, Inc. (Live)', 'Leper Messiah (Live)' and 'Ride the Lightning (Live)'), Le Boule Noire, Paris on 11 June 2003 ('Motorbreath (Live)') and Le Trabendo, Paris on 11 June 2003 ('Hit the Lights (Live)')

Producer: Bob Rock & Metallica
Live tracks recorded and mixed by: Mike Gillies
Release date: 12 January 2004
Chart placings: US: did not chart, UK: 42
Label: Elektra (US), Vertigo (UK)

Metallica's second EP and the penultimate release from the *St. Anger* album. The six live tracks which feature are all pulled from a day of three shows in France – ahead of the *Summer Sanitarium 2003* tour – billed as the 'hottest day in French history' in the CDS liner notes.

'The Unnamed Feeling' (7:10)

'The Four Horsemen (Live)' (5:30)
The first song from the Le Bataclan set, and they come crashing straight in – the sound is tight and studio-like. Lars' snare pops perfectly and Hetfield's vocal is right in your ears and clear as day. Hetfield asks the crowd to sing the choruses, but you can barely hear them over the mayhem. They do come to the fore during a brief breakdown, though. Kirk's solo is, unfortunately, a little hidden in the live mix, but if you strain, you can hear it, and he's playing it well. A 'bonjour' from Hetfield leads to a crowd fade-out.

'Damage, Inc. (Live)' (4:59)
This is the final track from the short(ish), nine-song Le Bataclan set. Kirk's solo from 2:24 is absolutely insane and more audible this time.

'Leper Messiah (Live)' (6:24)
The second track from Le Bataclan (weirdly positioned here). Trujillo's bass throbs during the intro sections – up in the mix – but Hetfield sounds like he struggles in the first verse. In fact, he sounds a little like he can't be bothered at times and is slightly out of tune too – reinforcing my previous album filler comment. His bandmates rescue him from the breakdown at 3:39 and pick up the pace well – another tremendous Kirk solo too. There's a quirky dead stop at 5:38, slightly delaying the track's end.

'Motorbreath (Live)' (3:13)
Dedicated to the road crew for 'making three shows in one day happen', Lars launches into an improvised intro before Hetfield cackles over his own riff. This was the encore from the first show that day.

'Ride the Lightning (Live)' (7:31)
This penultimate track (before the encore) at the Bataclan gig starts with a loose jam and Hetfield introducing the band – most notably the 'newest Metallica family member, Mr Robert Trujillo'. A full rendition is then

unleashed after Hetfield admits that they 'haven't played this song in a while – love it, baby!' It's a great version to be fair.

'Hit the Lights (Live)' (4:10)
The only track on this EP to come from the final show of the day in Paris – Le Trabendo – and it's the final one of that day too. Rather apt as it's one of the very first songs they ever played live. Still given as much gusto as in those early 1980s days and still with two Kirk solos.

Six Feet Down Under (2010)
Personnel:
Kirk Hammett: guitars
James Hetfield: guitars, vocals
Jason Newsted: bass
Robert Trujillo: bass
Lars Ulrich: drums
Recorded at: Festival Hall, Melbourne, Australia on 4 May 1989 ('Eye Of The Beholder (Live)' and '...And Justice For All (Live)'), the Entertainment Centre, Perth, Australia on 8 April 1993 ('Through the Never (Live)'), the National Tennis Centre, Melbourne, Australia on 4 April 1993 ('The Unforgiven (Live)'), the Entertainment Centre, Perth on 11 April 1998 ('Low Man's Lyric (Acoustic) (Live)'), the Entertainment Centre, Perth on 12 April 1998 ('Devil's Dance (Live)', the Entertainment Centre, Sydney, Australia on 21 January 2004 ('Frantic (Live)') and the Entertainment Centre, Brisbane, Australia on 19 January 2004 ('Fight Fire With Fire (Live)')
All songs 'fixed' (wherever possible) by: Kent Matcke
Release date: 20 September 2010
Chart placings: did not chart
Label: Universal Music

Released as a promo tool for the 'Down Under' leg of the 2010 'World Magnetic' tour, this neat (eventual two CD) set pulls performances from similar legs going back to the 'Damaged Justice' tour from 1989.

'Eye of the Beholder (Live)' (6:32)
It's almost impossible to get past the god-awful, tinny sound of this live recording – the audio swings between the speakers and there's even some up close and personal crowd conversation. This is proper bootleg stuff but probably should NOT have been included (although the crowd do sound like they're having a damned good time). This was the fifth track of this particular night at Melbourne's Festival Hall.

'...And Justice for All (Live)' (9:53)
The terrible live sound continues into a full rendition of the album title classic. There's more crowd eavesdropping to be heard – clearly, their steady

rise to fame did not involve shelling out on decent recording equipment at this stage. This was the final track of the set (before the encore) at Melbourne's Festival Hall.

'Through the Never (Live)' (3:40)

The awful sound continueth – sounding like (as the two former) it's been recorded on a past its sell-by date mic, wedged at the bottom of a trash can. Thank the lord it's 'never' and that it doesn't go on 'forever'. This was the 11th track of the night at Perth's Entertainment Centre.

'The Unforgiven (Live)' (7:02)

At last, we get a marginally better sound. This is 1993, after all and the band is at its peak. Some investment has finally been made. Hetfield's vocals are disappointingly lost, however – the only saving grace is a nice fat drum sound. This was the seventh track of the night at Melbourne's National Tennis Centre.

'Low Man's Lyric (Live)' (7:00)

Hetfield plays with the crowd before the intro and his vocal is, this time, loud and proud. A rare moment of relative calm among the usual on-the-road carnage. This was the first encore track at their return to Perth's Entertainment Centre in 1998.

'Devil's Dance (Live)' (5:49)

There's more crowd banter and some Lars riffing before Newsted drives home the opening riff. Kirk also joins in the riffing with some suitable screeching here and there from his own instrument. This was the seventh track of their second consecutive (return) night at Perth's Entertainment Centre.

'Frantic (Live)' (7:46)

Yet more improvisation of what sounds like 'Some Kind of Monster' kicks things off here, with Hetfield cajoling the crowd by asking how many have the *St. Anger* album. His vocals are lost again throughout, though, with Lars' tom sound the only real noticeable highlight.

The sixth track of the night at Sydney's Entertainment Centre.

'Fight Fire With Fire (Live)' (5:09)

The introductory riff is deathly, and Hetfield's vocal is exactly like the recorded version. Again, he goads the crowd before the lead break section. The pick of the bunch from this motley crew – each band member shining – Metallica as we know and love at last.

The opening track of the show at Brisbane's Entertainment Centre.

Six Feet Down Under Part 2 (2010)

Personnel:
Kirk Hammett: guitars
James Hetfield: guitars, vocals
Robert Trujillo: bass
Lars Ulrich: drums
Recorded at: the Entertainment Centre, Brisbane, Australia on 16 October 2010
('Blackened (Live)' and 'Master of Puppets (Live)'), the Vector Arena, Aukland,
New Zealand on 14 October 2010 ('Ride the Lightning (Live)'), the Acer Arena,
Sydney, Australia on 18 September 2010 ('The Four Horsemen (Live)' and 'Fade
to Black (Live)'), The Rod Laver Arena, Melbourne, Australia on 15 September
2010 ('Welcome Home (Sanitarium) (Live)'), the Entertainment Centre, Brisbane
on 18 October 2010 ('...And Justice For All (Live)') and the CBS Canterbury
Arena, Christchurch, New Zealand on 22 September 2010 ('Damage, Inc. (Live)')
Recorded and mixed by: Mike Gillies
Release date: 15 November 2010
Chart placings: did not chart
Label: Vertigo

All the tracks on this 'Part 2' are taken from the actual Down Under legs of
the 'World Magnetic' tour. The digipack CD sleeve came with a handy space
to insert CD one for all Metalli-faithful.

'Blackened (Live)' (6:27)

The live sound is much improved and the band are tight, particularly in the
opening sections. Trujillo picks up Newsted's previous backing vocal duties
incredibly well. This was the 13th track of the opening night of a three-night
run at Brisbane's Entertainment Centre.

'Ride the Lightning (Live)' (7:10)

A rare-ish outing for this second album classic, handled well by Hetfield, who
scales the heady heights of the vocal pitching. The crowd are in fine form here,
belting out the second half of the chorus and joining in with 'heys' during the
instrumental section – which features Kirk on top form as usual. This was the
third track of the second consecutive night at Auckland's Vector Arena.

'The Four Horsemen (Live)' (5:20)

Some great crowd interaction from Hetfield throughout here and another fine end
solo from Kirk. This was the seventh track of the night at Sydney's Acer Arena.

'Welcome Home (Sanitarium) (Live)' (6:23)

An extremely mellow intro – from all band members – bleeds into its more
usual frantic finale from 3:40. This was the ninth track of the first night of a
two-night run at Melbourne's Rod Laver Arena.

'Master of Puppets (Live)' (8:23)
A second full-length version of an early album title track and the crowd participates wonderfully during the solo section. The effects on Hetfield's vocals pre-solo and, at the end, make this a worthy addition. This was the 12th track of the first night at Brisbane's Entertainment Centre.

'...And Justice for All (Live)' (9:08)
The sound quality is poor again during the intro but thankfully bursts fully into life again from 59 seconds in – as if someone has suddenly nudged a mic into its proper place. This completes the inclusion of full versions of the first three album track titles; a nice addition, particularly if you were lucky enough to have been at any of the shows on the tour. This was the tenth track of the second night of the three nights of shows at Brisbane's Entertainment Centre.

'Fade to Black (Live)' (7:33)
The acoustic guitar has a lovely warm sound to it during the intro and Kirk's lead playing is clear and bright – crowd singing along to its melody in unison. There's a teasing hang at 4:01, where Hetfield asks the crowd if they can 'feel it?' before the song builds to its ultimate finale. This was the fifth track of the night at Sydney's Acer Arena.

'Damage, Inc. (Live)' (5:25)
The original reverse guitar sound kicks off this final track of the Down Under set – a fine way to finish – and another raucous rendition of this *Puppetz* closer. This was the 13th track of the second consecutive night at Christchurch's CBS Canterbury Arena.

Lulu (2011)
Personnel:
Kirk Hammett: guitars
James Hetfield: guitars, vocals
Lou Reed: guitars, continuum, vocals
Robert Trujillo: bass
Lars Ulrich: drums
Sarth Calhoun: electronics
Jenny Scheinman: violin, viola and string arrangements
Megan Gould: violin
Ron Lawrence: viola
Marika Hughes: cello
Ulrich Maas: cello on 'Little Dog' and 'Frustration'
Rob Wasserman: stand up electric bass on 'Junior Dad'
Jessica Troy: viola on 'Junior Dad'
Recorded at: HQ, San Rafael, California between April and June 2011

Producer: Lou Reed, Metallica, Hal Willner & Greg Fidelman
Release date: 1 November 2011
Chart placings: US: 13, UK: 36
Label: Warner Bros. (US), Vertigo (UK)
All songs on this album are written by Lou Reed & Metallica

The idea of a concept album does actually lend itself to much of Metallica's progressive blend of modern metal, but whether that concept should have been Lou Reed's re-imagining of Frank Wedekind's horrific sex tragedies is a question long pondered by many fans.

It could and should have been a great project and at times, reaches some pleasing heights; the problem is Reed's awful vocals constantly grating against an often vibrant-sounding band. If that was the aim, then they pull it off brilliantly but taken as a whole, it's a very hard listen. Often sounding like two completely different competing ideas, it's hard to get a grasp of what's really going on – save Reed's more than exposing and direct lyrics.

It's unsettling, disturbing and leaves a nasty and long-lasting impression on the listener. Like watching a horror movie alone on Halloween night and having to go to bed on your own straight after. You long for the end and morning's early light soon after the end of track one.

Reviews weren't all bad however. Indeed *Rolling Stone*'s David Fricke described the partnership as 'a raging union of Reed's 1973 noir classic *Berlin* and Metallica's *Master of Puppets,* with Lars rebuffing any stinging complaints about the project and its unusual premise by reminding folks that 'in 1984 when hardcore Metallica fans heard acoustic guitars on 'Fade to Black', there was a nuclear meltdown in the metal community'.

The album artwork depicts an image of a female mannequin – head and torso only – with *Lulu* scrawled across its front in blood. Similar imagery is depicted throughout the inlay, with an Anton Corbijn shot of the band with Reed himself seated around a *Load*-esque table on the back cover.

'Brandenburg Gate' (4:19)
The acoustic guitar of the intro makes this sounds like a ballad at first – until the vocals begin that is. 'I would cut my legs and tits off when I think of Boris Karloff and Kinski in the dark of the moon' – OK then, Mr Reed. We soon know that Metallica are also in the room as they kick in with Hetfield repeating the 'small town girl' refrain.

'The View' (5:17)
Lars announces things with a lazy drum pattern, closely followed by the guitars, which practically repeat over and over. The bass is dirty and so are Reed's lyrics: 'I have no morals; some think me cheap and someone who despises the normalcy of heartbreak'.

The real Metallica stand up again from 1:59 as Hetfield takes over before it takes an even darker turn from 4:15 – riff drilling down to a solo until the main pattern returns to take us to the end.

'Pumping Blood' (7:24)

A haunting, almost serene-sounding guitar soon makes way for a pounding kick drum, then another deathly riff. At 2:06, we get a dead stop and then Reed riffs over a clean guitar and some improvised Lars fills until a new theme is introduced. Lars complements it with increasing tom runs until his snare drum takes the track in yet another direction. Here lies the crux of this album – to-ing and fro-ing from one dark section to another. Just as you think it's settled, it takes another surprising turn.

'Mistress Dread' (6:51)

We get the real Metallica again – a speed riff and drums – soon after some organ and feedback. Reed's awful mumbling sounds are really at odds with the music here: 'I'm a woman who likes men, but this is something else. I've never felt such stirrings, I feel like I was someone else.' Go figure? A painful listen.

'Iced Honey' (4:36)

A 'one, two, three' count from Reed starts off a fairly catchy verse for once. Catchy if not for his continued toneless delivery. At least Hetfield peppers things with the track's title at points, as well as providing some much-needed backing vocals towards the end.

'Cheat on Me' (11:26)

Another dark – very dark – turn, yet we begin with an almost peaceful string and mournful guitar lament. This carries on for over a minute and a half before the bass comes in. At 3:06, the relentless Reed resumes, depicting a tale of the self-loathing woman the album's named after. Hetfield supplies more backing vocals as the track unfolds, with Lars steadily building with the drums. About five minutes too long ...

'Frustration' (8:34)

After a minute of excruciating improvised guitar scratching, a great riff kicks in – soon ruined by Reed's spoken vocal delivery. From 2:28, a completely improvised section begins with Lars riffing over Reed's, 'I want so much to hurt you, marry me, I want you as my wife'. The guitar riff then resumes for a while until dropping out at 4:54 and leaving Reed alone until kicking back in a little later, faster this time and building to a thankful end.

'Little Dog' (8:01)

The first four-and-a-half minutes feature Reed's disgusting vocal – 'a puny body and a tiny dick, a little dog can make you sick' – over a depressing acoustic guitar and distant electric feedback, until Lars brings in some soft toms, barely shifting the dynamics. Another track that is about eight minutes too long ...

'Dragon' (11:08)
Keeping in vein with the previous track, this time over some improvised electric lead, Reed spouts more profanities until the full band kick in at 2:47. The same riff then loops, stopping for a brief, messy solo from 4:55, before continuing again in an almost hypnotic cycle over Reed's constant rants: 'The winner in heartbreak, the winner in caring, the winner in every miniscule method of wearing your heart on your sleeve.'

'Junior Dad' (19:29)
A mood-setting cello and strings introduce a country-style swing, setting up another ballad feel for this lengthy closer to the set. Lars' repeated snare and tom stabs at the end of the verse cycles start to sound like an unusual friendly companion until 4:22, when they peter out to allow Reed to assume the lead again over the bed of strings until 6:42, when Lars resumes. This continues until 10:44, when everything drops out, leaving just the strings, which drone on to the track's conclusion. A surprisingly peaceful end to an album full of dark and brooding horror.

Beyond Magnetic (2011)
Personnel:
Kirk Hammett: guitars
James Hetfield: guitars, vocals
Robert Trujillo: bass
Lars Ulrich: drums
Recorded at: Sound City, Van Nuys, Shangri La, Malibu, and HQ, San Rafael, California between April 2007 and March 2008
Producer: Rick Rubin
Release date: 13 December 2011
Chart placings: did not chart
Label: Blackened Recordings
All songs are written by Hetfield/Ulrich/Hammett/Trujillo.

Recorded during the original *Death Magnetic* sessions, these tracks were released digitally at first, then subsequently made available on CD and vinyl.

'Hate Train' (6:59)
The main riff kicks in after a flourish of guitar and drum stabs – a cool lead break played over the intro proper before the main song starts with a trademark Hetfield growl. A clean section from 2:19 introduces the chorus sections, before returning to the rage of the verses. The breakdown from 4:22,

complete with solo, is very reminiscent of the *Kill 'Em All* days, keeping in theme with the overall *Death Magnetic* vibe.

'Just a Bullet Away' (7:11)
A live feel count in at the start soon makes way for a *Black Album* 'Don't Tread on Me' main riff and vocal melody. The chorus sections are peppered with some pinpoint Lars drum fills round the kit, which dovetails perfectly back into the main riff. At 3:59, a dead stop for three seconds introduces a Cliff Burton-esque clean section with duelling melodic guitars. Lars then pounds back into the feature riff to introduce a Kirk solo and final verse/ chorus progression.

'Hell and Back' (6:57)
More clean guitar bleeds into a scything riff at the start here, then an almost muted strum ushers in verse one. The constant pound of Lars' kick drum gives the pre-chorus a real bite and what sounds like the end of the track at 3:49 actually kicks off a new section, with a building riff leading to a Kirk solo and final chorus round.

'Rebel of Babylon' (8:01)
The darkness of the intro brings in a Hetfield vocal which sounds clear and exposed – like he's in the room – before the main riff kicks in. There's an impressive fury on the guitars in the verse sections and Hetfield lets his 'tonight' ring out effectively over a shifting riff into the choruses. There's a medley feel about this, similar to the 'Mercyful Fate' track from *Garage Inc.*, particularly from 3:52 when an extended instrumental/solo section continues until 6:23 before a final verse/chorus run.

The 30th Anniversary Celebration (2012)
Personnel:
Kirk Hammett: guitars
James Hetfield: guitars, vocals
Robert Trujillo: bass
Lars Ulrich: drums
Recorded at: the Fillmore Theatre, San Francisco, California on 9 and 10 December 2011
Recorded by: Mike Gillies
Release date: 14 May 2012
Chart placings: did not chart
Label: Warner Bros

An exclusive 7" vinyl single included with issues of 'So What! The 30th Anniversary Event', *Metal Hammer* and Metallica Club magazines.

'So What (Live)' (7:31)

Hetfield tells the crowd a story from the younger days when they would play this track with their mates to piss off their neighbours, before introducing Animal from Anti-Nowhere League himself, who then demonstrates exactly why they offended all those people years ago. He hadn't lost the evil gravel in his voice and Kirk played a blistering solo on the night.

'Through the Never (Live)' (4:39)

One (Awards Show Rehearsal Version) (2014)

Personnel:
Kirk Hammett: guitars
James Hetfield: guitars, vocals
Robert Trujillo: bass
Lars Ulrich: drums
Lang Lang: piano
Recorded at: East West Studios, Los Angeles, California on 23 January 2014
Mixed by: Greg Fidelman and Mike Gillies
Release date: 11 February 2014
Chart placings: did not chart
Label: We're Only In It For The Music

Featuring Grammy Cultural Ambassador to China and classical pianist Lang Lang, this was recorded for a performance at the 56th Annual Grammy Awards.

'One (Awards Show Rehearsal Verson) (with Lang Lang)' (5:55)

Lang Lang riffs over the gunfire of the intro and again prior to the 'darkness imprisoning me' section, also adding some nice melodic touches to the verse sections throughout.

Lords of Summer (2014)

Personnel:
Kirk Hammett: guitars
James Hetfield: guitars, vocals
Robert Trujillo: bass
Lars Ulrich: drums
Recorded at: HQ, San Rafael, California ('Lords of Summer (First Pass Version)') and Sonisphere, Rome, Italy on 1 July 2014 ('Lords of Summer (Live at Rock in Rome)')
Producer: Hetfield & Ulrich ('First Pass Version') and recorded and mixed by Mike Gillies ('Live at Rock in Rome' version)
Release date: 20 June 2014
Chart placings: did not chart
Label: Blackened Recordings

Released initially as a standalone digital single (First Pass Version), then later as a 12" version also featuring the live cut.

'Lords of Summer (First Pass Version)' (Hetfield/Ulrich/Trujillo) (8:20)
After an extended intro, Lars brings in the first verse with a wave of double kick drum playing. There's heavy doses of 'Horsemen' and 'No Remorse' here – most notably in the lyrics – and an extended solo section, after a brief breakdown at 4:23. A telling Trujillo co-writing credit, minus Kirk.

'Lords of Summer (Live at Rock in Rome)' (8:48)

Blackened 2020 (2020)
Personnel:
Kirk Hammett: guitars
James Hetfield: guitars, vocals
Robert Trujillo: bass
Lars Ulrich: drums
Recorded: during the 2020 Covid-19 lockdowns
Release date: 15 May 2020
Chart placings: did not chart
Label: Blackened Recordings

'Blackened 2020' (5:32)
Recorded in isolation during the height of the 2020 Covid-19 lockdowns, its ballad-esque swing and almost hushed Hetfield vocal prove beyond all doubt that this is a love song to our battered 'Mother Earth' after all. It works on all levels, particularly the little guitar flourishes in the original call and response sections and Kirk's excellent, soulful solo playing.

Part Six: The Singles Club

'Jump in the Fire' b/w **'Seek & Destroy (Live)'** and **'Phantom Lord (Live)'**
Released: 20 January 1984
Chart placings: US: did not chart, UK: did not chart.

'Whiplash (Special Neckbrace Remix)' b/w **'Jump in the Fire', 'Seek & Destroy (Live)'** and **'Phantom Lord (Live)'**
Released: 23 January 1984
Chart placings: US: did not chart, UK: did not chart.
This remix of Whiplash was commissioned by the American label Megaforce Records as an early tool to help promote the debut album and sounds – to my ears – exactly like the album version. Maybe the drums are slightly more pronounced and there is potentially a little bit more effect on Hetfield's vocals, but apart from that, I don't hear it.

'Creeping Death' b/w **'Am I Evil?', 'Blitzkrieg', 'Jump in the Fire', 'Seek & Destroy (Live)'** and **'Phantom Lord (Live)'**
Released: 23 November 1984
Chart placings: US: did not chart, UK: did not chart.

'Master of Puppets' b/w **'Welcome Home (Sanitarium) (Edit)'**
Released: 2 July 1986
Chart placings: US: did not chart, UK: did not chart.

'Harvester of Sorrow' b/w **'Breadfan** and **'The Prince'**
Released: 28 August 1988
Chart placings: US: did not chart, UK: 20.

'Eye of the Beholder' b/w **'Breadfan'**
Released: 30 October 1988
Chart placings: US: did not chart, UK: did not chart.

'One' b/w **'The Prince', 'For Whom the Bell Tolls (Live)', 'Welcome Home (Sanitarium) (Live)', 'Seek & Destroy (Live)', 'Breadfan', 'One (Demo)'** and **'Creeping Death (Live)'**
Released: 10 January 1989
Chart placings: US: 35, UK: 13.

'Enter Sandman' b/w **'Stone Cold Crazy', 'Enter Sandman (Demo)'** and **'Holier Than Thou (Work in Progress)'**
Released: 29 July 1991
Chart placings: US: 16, UK: 5.

'The Unforgiven' b/w 'Killing Time', 'The Unforgiven (Demo)' and 'So What'

Released: 28 October 1991
Chart placings: US: 35, UK: 15.

'Nothing Else Matters' b/w 'Enter Sandman (Live)', 'Harvester of Sorrow (Live)' and 'Nothing Else Matters (Demo)'

Released: 20 April 1992
Chart placings: US: 34, UK: 6.

'Wherever I May Roam' b/w 'Fade to Black (Live)', 'Wherever I May Roam (Demo)' and 'Last Caress/Am I Evil?/Battery (Live)'

Released: 19 October 1992
Chart placings: US: 82, UK: 25.

'Sad but True' b/w 'So What', 'Harvester of Sorrow (Live)', 'Nothing Else Matters (Elevator Version)', 'Creeping Death (Live)', 'Sad but True (Demo)', 'Nothing Else Matters (Live)' and 'Sad but True (Live)'

Released: 8 February 1993
Chart placings: US: 98, UK: 20.

If ever you were to find yourself in an elevator going up to the top floor of a swanky office for an important boardroom meeting with Metallica, their version of 'Nothing Else Matters' included here might be your accompanying soundtrack. Hushed, with warm strings and played on – what sounds like – a twelve-string guitar. Hetfield croons it like a lullaby and it's actually quite beautiful. Film soundtrack fodder and an early nod to the classical future of *S&M*.

'One (Live)' b/w 'One', 'One (Demo)', 'Whiplash (Live)', 'For Whom the Bell Tolls (Live)' and 'Last Caress (Live)'

Released: 11 April 1994
Chart placings: US: did not chart, UK: did not chart.

'Until it Sleeps' b/w 'Overkill', '2 X 4 (Live)', 'F.O.B.D. (aka 'Until it Sleeps' – early 'writing in progress' version)', 'Kill/Ride Medley (Live)' and 'Until it Sleeps (Herman Melville Mix)'

Released: 21 May 1996
Chart placings: US: 10, UK: 5.

The 'early' take of 'Until it Sleeps' here features a surprising eight hi-hat count in from Lars and absolutely no lyrics whatsoever – just 'hey heys' and 'nah nahs' from Hetfield. The bulk of the song is there, however (including a short guitar solo) and it's an interesting fly-on-the-wall snapshot of their writing and recording process.

The Herman Melville Mix sounds like some sort of industrial dance track and nothing like the original at all. The only similarity is a few of the lyrics are repeated over the dancey and often excruciating bed of noise.

'Hero of the Day' b/w **'Kill/Ride Medley (Live)', 'Overkill', 'Damage Case', 'Hero of the Day (Outta B-Sides Mix)', 'Stone Dead Forever', 'Too Late Too Late'** and **'Mouldy' (aka 'Hero of the Day' – early demo version)**
Released: 10 September 1996
Chart placings: US: 60, UK: 17.
Barely any 'hey heys' or 'nah nahs' at all in the early (Mouldy) version of 'Hero of the Day' here. Not even any 'mama they try and break mes' either. Again the majority of the final song (and solo) is there though.

'Mama Said' b/w **'King Nothing (Live)', 'Whiplash (Live)', 'Mama Said (Edit)', 'So What (Live)', 'Creeping Death (Live)', 'Mama Said (Early Demo Version)'** and **'Ain't My Bitch (Live)'**
Released: 25 November 1996
Chart placings: US: did not chart, UK: 19.
The 'radio' edit of 'Mama Said' here kicks in straight away with the vocals, no mournfully strummed guitar intro. That's about the only 'edit' I can hear, anyway.

'King Nothing' b/w **'Ain't My Bitch (Live)'**
Released: 7 January 1997
Chart placings: US: 90, UK: did not chart.

'The Memory Remains' b/w **'For Whom the Bell Tolls (Haven't Heard It Yet Mix)', 'Fuel for Fire (Work in Progress with Different Lyrics)', 'Memory (Demo)', 'King Nothing (Tepid Mix)'** and **'The Outlaw Torn (Unencumbered by Manufacturing Restrictions Version)'**
Released: 11 November 1997
Chart placings: US: 28, UK: 13.
Similar to the 'Until it Sleeps' remix previously mentioned, you certainly wish you hadn't 'heard it yet' after just a few seconds into the 'For Whom the Bell Tolls' reworking here. The tolling bell is about the only resemblance to the original. An 'if it ain't broke, don't fix it' ethos should definitely have been employed.
There's a 'funk' to the 'King Nothing' remix and some nice spacey effects on the bass. The 'Outlaw Torn' version goes on for about a minute longer and doesn't fade – not really worth the long wait.

'The Unforgiven II' b/w **'The Thing That Should Not Be (Live)', 'Helpless (Live)', 'The Four Horsemen (Live)', 'Of Wolf and Man**

(Live)', 'The Memory Remains (Live)', 'King Nothing (Live)', 'No Remorse (Live)', 'Am I Evil? (Live)' and **'The Unforgiven II (Demo)'**
Released: 24 February 1998
Chart placings: US: 59, UK: 15.

'Fuel' b/w **'Sad but True (Live)', 'Nothing Else Matters (Live)', 'Wherever I May Roam (Live)', 'One (Live)', 'Until it Sleeps (Live)', 'Fuel (Live)'** and **'Fuel (Demo)'**
Released: 22 June 1998
Chart placings: US: did not chart, UK: 31.

'Turn the Page' b/w **'Bleeding Me (Live)', 'Stone Cold Crazy (Live)', 'The Wait (Live)', 'Damage, Inc. (Live)'** and **'Fuel (Video)'**
Released: 16 November 1998
Chart placings: US: did not chart, UK: did not chart.

'Whiskey in the Jar' b/w **'Blitzkrieg (Live)', 'The Prince (Live)', 'The Small Hours (Live)', 'Killing Time (Live)', 'Last Caress/Green Hell (Live)', 'Whiskey in the Jar (Live)', 'The Wait (Live)', 'Electronic Press Kit Pt. 1'** and **'Electronic Press Kit Pt. 2'**
Released: 1 February 1999
Chart placings: US: did not chart, UK: 29.

'Die, Die My Darling' b/w **'Sabbra Cadabra (Live)', 'Mercyful Fate (Live)', 'Turn the Page (Video)'** and **'Whiskey in the Jar (Video)'**
Released: 7 June 1999
Chart placings: US: did not chart, UK: did not chart.

'Nothing Else Matters (Live)' b/w **'For Whom the Bell Tolls (Live)', '-Human (Live)'** and **'Nothing Else Matters (Video)'**
Released: 22 November 1999
Chart placings: US: did not chart, UK: did not chart.

'No Leaf Clover (Live)' b/w **'No Leaf Clover (Slice & Dice Video)', 'S&M Documentary Pt. 1', 'S&M Documentary Pt. 2', 'S&M Documentary Pt. 3', 'One (Live)', 'Enter Sandman (Live)', 'No Leaf Clover (Video)', Photo Gallery/Album Lyrics** and **Metallica Screensaver**
Released: 20 March 2000
Chart placings: US: 74, UK: did not chart.

'I Disappear' b/w **'I Disappear (Instrumental)'**
Released: 26 June 2000
Chart placings: US: 76, UK: 35.

'St. Anger' b/w **'Commando'**, **'Today Your Love, Tomorrow the World'**, **'Now I Wanna Sniff Some Glue'**, **'Cretin Hop'** and **'We're a Happy Family'**
Released: 23 June 2003
Chart placings: US: did not chart, UK: 9.
Metallica recorded the Ramones' '53rd & 3rd' track as part of a Rob Zombie tribute album entitled *We're a Happy Family*, released on 11 February 2003. As part of the sessions at HQ in December 2003, they also had fun cutting some other rough and ready versions – particularly their take on 'We're a Happy Family' – as part of their own tribute, which is tongue-in-cheekily dubbed 'Garbage Days Revisited' on the Metallica website. It's more recording session insight for the diehards out there.

'Frantic' b/w **'Blackened (Live – Download Festival)'**, **'Harvester of Sorrow (Live – Download Festival)'**, **'No Remorse (Live – Download Festival)'**, **'Welcome Home (Sanitarium) (Live – Download Festival)'**, **'Frantic (UNKLE Reconstruction – Artificial Confidence)'**
Released: 15 September 2003
Chart placings: US: did not chart, UK: 16.
The UNKLE Reconstruction mix of 'Frantic' runs a similar course to the 'Until it Sleeps (Herman Melville Mix)' previously mentioned – a few looped lyrics over some industrial-sounding echoey effects – not really much to see here.

'Some Kind of Monster' b/w **'The Four Horsemen (Live)'**, **'Damage, Inc. (Live)'**, **'Leper Messiah (Live)'**, **'Motorbreath (Live)'**, **'Ride the Lightning (Live)'**, **'Hit the Lights (Live)'** and **'Some Kind of Monster (Edit)'**
Released: 13 July 2004
Chart placings: US: did not chart, UK: did not chart.
No lumbering two-minute intro to the 'edit' of 'Some Kind of Monster' here; in fact, it's cut almost exactly in half – 4:18 instead of an ear-bashing 8:25. A single version that works this time around.

'The Day That Never Comes' b/w **'No Remorse (Live)'**
Released: 21 August 2008
Chart placings: US: 31, UK: 19.

'All Nightmare Long' b/w **'Wherever I May Roam (Live)'**, **'Master of Puppets (Live)'**, **'Blackened (Live)'**, **'Seek & Destroy (Live)'**, **'Rock Im Park 'Container' Rehearsal'** and **'Berlin Magnetic (Documentary)'**
Released: 15 December 2008
Chart placings: US: did not chart, UK: did not chart.

'Broken, Beat, & Scarred' b/w **'Broken, Beat, & Scarred (Live)', 'The End of the Line (Live)', 'Stone Cold Crazy (Live)', 'Of Wolf and Man (Live)', 'Death Magnetic EPK/Promo Reel'** and **'The Day That Never Comes (Video)'**
Released: 3 April 2009
Chart placings: US: did not chart, UK: did not chart.

'One (Awards Show Rehearsal Version)' featuring **'One (Awards Show Rehearsal Version) (With Lang Lang)'**
Released: 11 February 2014
Chart placings: US: did not chart, UK: did not chart.

'Lords of Summer' b/w **'Lords of Summer (Live at Rock in Rome)'**
Released: 20 June 2014
Chart placings: US: did not chart, UK: did not chart.

'Hardwired'
Released: 18 August 2016
Chart placings: US: did not chart, UK: did not chart.

'Moth Into Flame'
Released: 26 September 2016
Chart placings: US: did not chart, UK: did not chart.

'Atlas, Rise!'
Released: 31 October 2016
Chart placings: US: did not chart, UK: did not chart.

'Now That We're Dead'
Released: 18 April 2017
Chart placings: US: did not chart, UK: did not chart.

'Spit Out the Bone (Radio Edit)'
Released: 14 November 2017
Chart placings: US: did not chart, UK: did not chart.

'Blackened 2020'
Released: 15 May 2020
Chart placings: US: did not chart, UK: did not chart.

'Lux Æterna'
Released: 28 November 2022
Chart placings: US: did not chart, UK: did not chart.

'Screaming Suicide'
Released: 19 January 2023
Chart placings: US: did not chart, UK: did not chart.

'If Darkness Had a Son'
Released: 1 March 2023
Chart placings: US: did not chart, UK: did not chart.

'72 Seasons'
Released: 30 March 2023
Chart placings: US: did not chart, UK: did not chart.

Jumping 'Out of' The Fire – An Afterword

As I reached the final stages of the writing process for this book in late April 2023, Metallica had recently made an appearance at the Microsoft Theater in Los Angeles on 16 December 2022 as part of their third All Within My Hands Helping Hands Concert and Auction. New M72 World Tour dates had already been pencilled in the diary across Europe, America and Canada for the rest of 2023 and into 2024, including two more headline appearances at the Download Festival in Castle Donington, UK, which took place on 8 and 10 June 2023. Headlining on both the Thursday and Saturday nights, the shows featured 'no repeat' set lists – a cute gimmick employed over two-night residencies from the early stages of the M72 tour – containing tracks from debut album, *Kill 'Em All*, right through to their latest *72 Seasons* release.

A band who are always working, always trying to please the fans. And what will the future hold? More shows and albums to come, without a doubt, I'm sure. Listening back through their catalogue has revealed many new hidden gems – not least the *Load* and *Reload* period when often, sat lurking in the shadows of their bigger and wealthier *Black Album* brother, I realised that at times I'd considered them less worthy than they are. This was wrong. They were surely destined to be set up for a fall; for how can anyone hope to replicate or better that stand-alone piece of work – but therein lies the key. They didn't try to. They also didn't resort back to plan A and attempt to emulate the thrashings of their past. Instead, they strove to create something new and, in part, encapsulated all that their music has to offer, in a more modern-sounding, yet less commercial flavour. They then threw the formula out of the window completely with the release of *St. Anger*, not to everyone's tastes for sure – but to theirs, it most certainly was.

All of the above and more is why I love this band so much. It's been hard to distance myself and be objective about their work during the course of my writing. I like some tracks and albums more than others and I have tried to be critical where I can – but more than anything I've tried to be fair.

They've always been there for me, at least, that's how it seems. Memories still burn clear of listening to Lars-esque ripped cassette copies of *Ride the Lightning* and *Master of Puppets* in the school classroom at lunchtime with my mates. The thrill of that first live concert on my sixteenth birthday and rushing to get the *Load* and *Reload* CDs from the record store on the day of release. There is nothing like it when you are a die-hard fan. Little to match the rapture of that first listen and the satisfaction when you grow to love it so well that you can practically recite it word for word, riff for riff, solo for piercingly true solo.

And I guess that's the beauty and power of music. One track or album will mean one thing to someone and something else to someone else. Memories and places in time can be so easily conjured with the flourish of a snare drum or hanging power chord. And these are the things that Metallica do exceptionally well. They are ornate masters of it – craftsmen and seasoned professionals. It's there in that headstrong debut and still very apparent all those years later in their latest, long-playing offering.

So, if you're interested in what a life-long fan thinks and makes of their music, then this book will speak to you. If you want to know how their music makes someone feel, what emotions it stirs and where it takes them, again, you may find it useful. It is not a biography and I do not claim to be the oracle on Metallica – that role is for someone else. I am a fan at heart and always will be. That sixteen-year-old lad stood in the field at Milton Keynes in 1993 hasn't really changed, but the music always has. And nothing else really matters anyway, does it ...? Thanks for listening/reading.

Bibliography

Books
Ewing, J. *Metallica – Heavy Metal's Biggest Band* (SevenOaks, 2015)
Strong, Martin C. *The Great Rock Discography 7ᵗʰ Edition* (Canongate Books Ltd, 2004)
Wall, M. *Enter Night – Metallica The Biography* (Orion, 2012)
So What! The Good, The Mad and The Ugly – The Official Metallica Illustrated Chronicle Edited by Steffan Chirazi (Hodder and Stoughton, 2004)

Internet
www.billboard.com
www.discogs.com
www.grammy.com/awards/56th-annual-grammy-awards
www.theguardian.com/news/2003/nov/21/guardianobituaries.artsobituaries
www.langlangofficial.com
www.metalica.com
www.metallica.fandom.com
www.nme.com/reviews/reviews-nme-7105-313073
www.officialcharts.com
www.rollingstone.com/music/music-album-reviews/st-anger-109159/amp

On Track series

Also available from Sonicbond

Jimi Hendrix – Emma Stott 978-1-78952-175-7
The Hollies – Andrew Darlington 978-1-78952-159-7
Horslips – Richard James 978-1-78952-263-1
The Human League and The Sheffield Scene –
Andrew Darlington 978-1-78952-186-3
The Incredible String Band – Tim Moon 978-1-78952-107-8
Iron Maiden – Steve Pilkington 978-1-78952-061-3
Joe Jackson – Richard James 978-1-78952-189-4
Jefferson Airplane – Richard Butterworth 978-1-78952-143-6
Jethro Tull – Jordan Blum 978-1-78952-016-3
Elton John in the 1970s – Peter Kearns 978-1-78952-034-7
Billy Joel – Lisa Torem 978-1-78952-183-2
Judas Priest – John Tucker 978-1-78952-018-7
Kansas – Kevin Cummings 978-1-78952-057-6
The Kinks – Martin Hutchinson 978-1-78952-172-6
Korn – Matt Karpe 978-1-78952-153-5
Led Zeppelin – Steve Pilkington 978-1-78952-151-1
Level 42 – Matt Philips 978-1-78952-102-3
Little Feat – Georg Purvis - 978-1-78952-168-9
Aimee Mann – Jez Rowden 978-1-78952-036-1
Joni Mitchell – Peter Kearns 978-1-78952-081-1
The Moody Blues – Geoffrey Feakes 978-1-78952-042-2
Motorhead – Duncan Harris 978-1-78952-173-3
Nektar – Scott Meze - 978-1-78952-257-0
New Order – Dennis Remmer - 978-1-78952-249-5
Nightwish – Simon McMurdo – 978-1-78952-270-9
Laura Nyro – Philip Ward 978-1-78952-182-5
Mike Oldfield – Ryan Yard 978-1-78952-060-6
Opeth – Jordan Blum 978-1-78-952-166-5
Pearl Jam – Ben L. Connor 978-1-78952-188-7
Tom Petty – Richard James 978-1-78952-128-3
Pink Floyd – Richard Butterworth 978-1-78952-242-6
The Police – Pete Braidis 978-1-78952-158-0
Porcupine Tree – Nick Holmes 978-1-78952-144-3
Queen – Andrew Wild 978-1-78952-003-3
Radiohead – William Allen 978-1-78952-149-8
Rancid – Paul Matts 989-1-78952-187-0
Renaissance – David Detmer 978-1-78952-062-0
REO Speedwagon – Jim Romag 978-1-78952-262-4
The Rolling Stones 1963-80 – Steve Pilkington 978-1-78952-017-0
The Smiths and Morrissey – Tommy Gunnarsson 978-1-78952-140-5
Spirit – Rev. Keith A. Gordon – 978-1-78952- 248-8
Stackridge – Alan Draper 978-1-78952-232-7

Status Quo the Frantic Four Years – Richard James 978-1-78952-160-3
Steely Dan – Jez Rowden 978-1-78952-043-9
Steve Hackett – Geoffrey Feakes 978-1-78952-098-9
Tears For Fears – Paul Clark - 978-178952-238-9
Thin Lizzy – Graeme Stroud 978-1-78952-064-4
Tool – Matt Karpe 978-1-78952-234-1
Toto – Jacob Holm-Lupo 978-1-78952-019-4
U2 – Eoghan Lyng 978-1-78952-078-1
UFO – Richard James 978-1-78952-073-6
Van Der Graaf Generator – Dan Coffey 978-1-78952-031-6
Van Halen – Morgan Brown – 9781-78952-256-3
The Who – Geoffrey Feakes 978-1-78952-076-7
Roy Wood and the Move – James R Turner 978-1-78952-008-8
Yes – Stephen Lambe 978-1-78952-001-9
Frank Zappa 1966 to 1979 – Eric Benac 978-1-78952-033-0
Warren Zevon – Peter Gallagher 978-1-78952-170-2
10CC – Peter Kearns 978-1-78952-054-5

Decades Series
The Bee Gees in the 1960s – Andrew Mon Hughes et al 978-1-78952-148-1
The Bee Gees in the 1970s – Andrew Mon Hughes et al 978-1-78952-179-5
Black Sabbath in the 1970s – Chris Sutton 978-1-78952-171-9
Britpop – Peter Richard Adams and Matt Pooler 978-1-78952-169-6
Phil Collins in the 1980s – Andrew Wild 978-1-78952-185-6
Alice Cooper in the 1970s – Chris Sutton 978-1-78952-104-7
Alice Cooper in the 1980s – Chris Sutton 978-1-78952-259-4
Curved Air in the 1970s – Laura Shenton 978-1-78952-069-9
Donovan in the 1960s – Jeff Fitzgerald 978-1-78952-233-4
Bob Dylan in the 1980s – Don Klees 978-1-78952-157-3
Brian Eno in the 1970s – Gary Parsons 978-1-78952-239-6
Faith No More in the 1990s – Matt Karpe 978-1-78952-250-1
Fleetwood Mac in the 1970s – Andrew Wild 978-1-78952-105-4
Fleetwood Mac in the 1980s – Don Klees 978-178952-254-9
Focus in the 1970s – Stephen Lambe 978-1-78952-079-8
Free and Bad Company in the 1970s – John Van der Kiste 978-1-78952-178-8
Genesis in the 1970s – Bill Thomas 978178952-146-7
George Harrison in the 1970s – Eoghan Lyng 978-1-78952-174-0
Kiss in the 1970s – Peter Gallagher 978-1-78952-246-4
Manfred Mann's Earth Band in the 1970s – John Van der Kiste 978178952-243-3
Marillion in the 1980s – Nathaniel Webb 978-1-78952-065-1
Van Morrison in the 1970s – Peter Childs - 978-1-78952-241-9
Mott the Hoople and Ian Hunter in the 1970s –
John Van der Kiste 978-1-78-952-162-7

Would you like to write for Sonicbond Publishing?

At Sonicbond Publishing we are always on the look-out for authors, particularly for our two main series:

On Track. Mixing fact with in depth analysis, the On Track series examines the work of a particular musical artist or group. All genres are considered from easy listening and jazz to 60s soul to 90s pop, via rock and metal.

On Screen. This series looks at the world of film and television. Subjects considered include directors, actors and writers, as well as entire television and film series. As with the On Track series, we balance fact with analysis.

While professional writing experience would, of course, be an advantage the most important qualification is to have real enthusiasm and knowledge of your subject. First-time authors are welcomed, but the ability to write well in English is essential.

Sonicbond Publishing has distribution throughout Europe and North America, and all books are also published in E-book form. Authors will be paid a royalty based on sales of their book.

Further details are available from www.sonicbondpublishing.co.uk. To contact us, complete the contact form there or email info@sonicbondpublishing.co.uk